Mods, Scooters & Memories
by Lucky

GY 65 CLUB Scooter Boys.

ISBN 10:0-9542932-1-5

ISBN 13: 978-0-9542932-1-5

EAN: 9780954293215

Life Force Books / Life Force Publishing. UK.

First Edition: 2019.

Format: Royal - Colour - Larger Print.

Mods, Scooters & Memories
by Lucky

GY65 CLUB Scooter Boys.

Credits: My memory of the times, places and names in the 60's is like the proverbial Swiss cheese! Huge "Thanks" to Pat Weller, Peter "Peewee" Rouse, Chris Baker-Pretty, Peter Allard, Brian Church, Bryan Bream, Henry Manguzi, Graham Hales and Graham Dallimore for their assistance in filling those gaps and/or supplying old photographs. Without their fantastic memories this book would have been nothing but a rough guide as my memories of those heady days were just as vague as faded photographs; but you just know that it was all good times! Also any other unnamed contributor who gave me details of their own personal experiences, or at least the ones they remembered best.

Foreword:
The mid-sixties, to be precise 1964 to 1967 were the most amazing times in the history of Great Britain, especially as far as being a teenager was concerned. It was such a privilege to be there for there were no other times as exciting for teenagers in the whole of the UK or Europe. It was a time of new ideas, new music, new fashions – thanks to bands like The Beatles – and discovery of new and uncharted grounds for teenagers across the globe. We broke free of the post-war drabness and created an adventurous attitude. That was later in the 70's temporarily

lost by the insanity of the era of the Punks, who, it seemed, were just hell bent on destroying everything and acting like zombies on Speed!

Being a teenager did not come without its problems though. Many older people looked down on us with disdain and disgust. The police victimised us and even some employers were less keen to take on a Mod: it seems that they either despised us for rebelling against "the norm", or maybe they were jealous! Either way, we were going to do "our thing", not theirs. Their attitude was the same as the 1% Rockers or 1% Mods that hurled abuse or even deck chairs at the "other lot", narrow-mindedness and ignorance. It's the same problem as Racism, but this time over fashion choice. We did not disrespect our elders, but many of us felt sorry for them because they just didn't understand us and didn't even try. My father never said much and now I realise that was probably because he was once a "teenage rebel" too. He just watched me from the sidelines, so to speak. As long as I was not dead he was happy for me to do my own thing and learn life's lessons and grow stronger from them.

The 1960's though was a special decade. It was rampant with change. The war years and "depression" afterwards, followed by industrial smog and more Labour/Conservative backlashes caused our parents to be quite depressed and, dare I say "dulled". The sixties opened up new trends, fashions and opportunities; a bit like a dull grey-green bush in winter followed by an explosion of blooms and colour in the summer.

What really happened in the "swinging sixties"? Sit back, relax and I'll tell you all about it: well, most, the bits I recalled and those that can be published!

MODS, SCOOTERS & The 1960's.
By 'Lucky' – an original GY 65 Club member and one of the first
few Mods in Gt Yarmouth in 1963.

Dancing with my sister's friend Maddy c.1966 at a Fancy Dress
Party – Fancy dress? Easy, stick a white Trilby on with my Italian
¾ Black Leather coat, hold a cigar and hey presto
"Gangster", job done!

Intro.

I wasn't always a Mod. In Gt. Yarmouth, when I was 14 to 16, there were still lots of Teddy Boys and "half-teds" (had a quiff hair, Elvis style) but wore drainpipe jeans and often rode motorbikes. Because they enjoyed Rock 'n' Roll most public thought that was why they were called "Rockers". However, some say that the true meaning came from the 'Rockers' inside the Motorcycle engines. I had my first pair of jeans then, like wearing cardboard tubes it was, they were so damned stiff! I can still see myself strolling into the Army Surplus Store in Great Yarmouth Market Place, on the West side, and buying them when I was 14-15. I felt so grown up. There I was, 1962, a mere 15 year-old strolling through the market place on Saturday, hands stuck firmly in the ultra-tight pockets and sporting my new leather jacket, feeling like I was no longer a kid. Three much older and much bigger Half-teds came towards me from the other direction, the chip stall end. As they approached they just gave each other a well-rehearsed nod and passed either side of me hooking their arms through mine to drag me backwards. My hands were stuck and I couldn't move. After a short drag, one punched me on the nose and unceremoniously dropped me on my backside. As I had been dragged off-balance I had no option but to sit or fall down on the cold market cobbles. My nose started to pour blood. After managing with a struggle to extract my hands from my jeans pockets, I found my handkerchief and caught the blood. The three stooges just stood there, looking at me, then each other, like they'd just achieved something or were waiting for applause. Not knowing the language of Moron, I decided to speak slowly in plain English, "There…" nodding directly to the punching moron and laughingly said, "I'm laughing about it... satisfied now?" Obviously not understanding, he looked at his mates, looked confused and they all walked off. Not a great first impression of my peers.

Here we go then, on the incredible and colourful journey through the Swinging Sixties, mainly from my own perspective, but I shall try to squeeze a couple of stories out of "the lads" to give it a wider perspective. Having discovered that I had massive memory loss from that era (more about that later), and then catching up with many of "the lads" at The Chalet Coffee Bar, I've managed to pinpoint a few events and even tag the year and season on most of them. To help me do this I made a Spreadsheet, divided into the years and seasons. Then I entered brief event titles in the timeline so as to rebuild my memories and give you a clearer picture of how it all kicked off in Great Yarmouth: please bear in mind that we were probably almost a year behind London at first, as Media was confined to motley newspapers and very, very little Television coverage of events pertaining to Mods! Only later, in terms of the fashion industry, did we end up literally two days behind London as our heroic fashion store owners made regular trips to buy the "just this minute out" designs we craved for.

Road Map

"In our day a Mod was a young person
who enjoyed fashion and scooters.
Nowadays a Mod is a extra *hack* on
bloody Minecraft!"
Lucky.

Chapter One

1963: Despite the early brush with the Moron clan, I stuck with the leather jacket until late '63. In fact, just aft er the Beatles were invented and hit the Great Yarmouth music scene with a bang. I had a leather jacket, faux-leather jeans and a leather tie; with my name on it... just in case I forgot who I was. Of course, I had a bike; a genuine bit-n-bobs "push-bike" with "cow-horn handle bars"; all the rage. It even had tassels hanging off the ends of the handlebars. Very "hip"! This was still the early sixties, the rock-and-roll era. On Sunday, June the 30th, I recall cycling past the ABC Theatre (and Cinema in winter) at the top of Regent Road. As I passed I saw four or five girls outside the Stage Door at the back. They were waving bits of paper and screaming intermittently, like a group of endangered Dodo's. Wondering what all the fuss was about, as this sort of weird behaviour thing had not been seen before, especially in sleepy Great Yarmouth (GY). I carried on cycling around the corner and onto Regent Road. I spied the sign on the front of the ABC theatre saying 'The Beatles'. "Oh." I thought to myself, "That's that new band that has the 'Love Me Do' hit in the charts. How odd those girls are that are screaming." This is when they started their first UK Tour, the first of a ten week series that rocketed them to fame and world-wide stardom. Those girls went unreported in the local rags, but later, when Beatle Mania really hit, there would be thousands of them all screaming their hearts out at John, George, Ringo and Paul. If you were lucky enough to have been there, Tickets for the show would cost between 4s/6d (around £2.89 today) to 9s/6d (£6.11). This was their first stop of The Beatles' Seaside Tour of Great Britain hosted by a new comedian, a chap called Ted Rodgers, later TV Game Show host. Other acts who accompanied The Beatles at the ABC Gt Yarmouth were The Brook Brothers, The Terry Young Combo, Erkey Grant, and Tommy Wallis and Beryl. Never heard of them? Neither had I.

Great Yarmouth, as it was generally called then but now just "Yarmuff", used to be a thriving and busy seaside resort in the summer with packed beaches, packed hotels and guest houses as well as caravan and camp sites. In our early teens, if you wanted to make "a couple of bob" (two shillings, or 2/-) you would head to Beach station early on a Saturday and offer to carry bags for the flocks of incoming holiday makers. That was hard work as they would really watch you struggle, being just a boy it was not easy to carry 4-6 cases at once. Those with business in mind made Barrows and took the biggest loads and did the most runs in a day, making far more than most. Great Yarmouth really did thrive with its two Piers, both with theatres, plus the ABC Regal and ABC Regent Cinema, The Aquarium Cinema, The Windmill Theatre and of course the Hippodrome Circus too. At one point someone reopened the old Empire Cinema, roughly in the middle of the seafront, and showed Musicals by day and Horror films at night. There was a lot happening and the atmosphere was vibrant. In the winter you could easily count the number of walkers on the beach on your fingers, but in the summertime it was packed tight with holiday makers. Many of these came from the midlands and industrial cities like Sheffield – then known world-wide for steel making, tools and steel cutlery of the highest order, nowadays known of course for…. Err? Well, moving on, these people arrived by

Coach, Train and some by car. Even the Scottish and Welsh came from far off exotic sounding places with unpronounceable names, many of the Welsh from villages or towns not far from the Welsh coast. That's how popular Great Yarmouth was. It was a mystery to us youngsters. Having seen the town in winter, and used to being ripped off in summer, we wondered why anyone would want to travel all that way to get there. As they say, "every cloud has a silver lining" and ours was the arrival of many young women from these far off places.

The girls of the sixties were a mixture of coy, hard to get and "Hey, are you interested boy?" This was the only time that we met girls with names like Agnes, Blodwen and Myfanwy, not to mention the Scots with their back to front names like Senga (Agnes in reverse!); Hmmm, I wonder what became of Senga; we were so in love for that fortnight, but of course, after two weeks she had to go home and young love fades away into deep space. Perhaps it was the letters that summertime lovers used to send each other then, you know, the ones with "SWALK" and "NORWICH" written all over the envelope, to name but two of the many acronyms. Little did we think about parents; I would imagine that many parents intercepted them and burned them before the lovelorn teenage girl could get a look in and then grounded their daughters until they were older! As a teenager I was completely naïve and hadn't got a clue what it all meant, let alone what parents thought. Now I'm a parent!

Great Yarmouth, or G.Y., as we called it, was awash with colour. From the many amusement arcades to the perfectly kempt gardens and flowering Waterways with its fairy-tale boats gliding holiday makers around the twisting canals, to the many fashions and trends that existed in those times; not just modern either as the older men on holidays "from t' midlands" used to wear traditional gear too, namely grey or fawn trousers, striped shirt with studded collar removed and a cream cloth cap; or cream summer hat, if "posh". Being young we often had nowhere to go with our holiday dates so would hang around the seafront amusement arcades, in one or two specific coffee bars or go for romantic strolls along the seafront promenade or by the colourful Waterways lights, going into the shelters for a kiss and a cuddle. Like I said, some girls were game, some were not, so half the time all you got was a kiss and a cuddle, however, I was still a virgin at 17, so were some of the girls, so any attempted sexual encounter was awkward, clumsy and, in retrospective, probably quite unexciting. Completely opposite of today's generations who it seems are starting at 9 and following pornography on smart phones whilst at High School! Yup, the sixties were much better: better to be in the dark than trying to imitate porn actors I say. At least we had a life, and it was a very active one at that! That summer of '63 saw an upturn in entertainment aimed for once at the younger generation with stars like Joe Brown & The Bruvvers, Mark Wynter, The Tornados, The Off-Keys, at Windmill and Rolf Harris. A fairly typical assortment for those days at a seaside resort.

Where Are They Now?
Many of my friends used to gather on Saturdays in the Kenya Coffee bar, above Palmers shop in the market place. Perhaps we'd move on to the Wimpy Bar, just past the Bloater shop on Regent Road and near what still is the most amazing (Uhum!) novelty and gift shop; it still exists today (2012 when this part was written) and sells all sorts of "stuff", you know, the sort that 20 years later you say "Whatever did I buy *that* crap for?!"

Readers from Great Yarmouth may recall another shop on Regent Road, more or less opposite that gift and novelty shop. It was a clothes shop which specialised in Indian clothing, Kaftans, cheesecloth shirts, women's dresses and the like. A tall Indian or

Pakistani (?) Man used to run it. He often stood outside and nodded, smiled or said hello to passers-by. After visiting the shop several times and buying odd shirts, he once invited me in for a chat. He had a girl working for him and asked her to make coffee then look after the shop while we sat at the counter and talked. He talked about life, philosophy and religions. He then said that if I came back in tomorrow he'd show me a book which belonged to his uncle. A very special book. The next day I did drop by and he showed me a book called "Koran", written in English. He gave me some story about how it was his Uncle's book , said I should take it, read it then return it. This I did. He then tried to persuade me that I could become a sort of missionary for Islam and go to India for training. The whole thing smelled rather fishy to me then and I returned the book saying that I was not interested. What little we knew then, eh?

Oh The Times They Are A Changing.
In 1962 I had just left Great Yarmouth College of Arts & Crafts after a two-year "Prelim" course. which I enjoyed, especially Silversmithing and Interior Design, but the options after leaving were few and also far away. Making the decision not to go far away, I had to look for work in the local area, and factory work paid more than shop or office work, so my search was on an I ended up, like many lost souls, in the clattering depths of Grouts Textiles Ltd.

As I said earlier, before the Mods (as we knew them) came with the Beatles and a whole new era of fashion and discovery, as well as teenage rebellions and new found expression. At that time – of The Beatles concert - I was still a leather clad rocker, of sorts, but the Beatles fashions looked so fresh, new and appealing. I became a convert in late '63, when the Beatles were in full swing and "invented" the collarless Beatle Jacket. They looked so cool, I had to get one, normal collars were just "so square". My new jacket was a blue and black kind of tweedy weave with slit pockets. The real novelty was the foam lining, yes "foam". A thin layer of foam was sewn between the outer fabric and swish shiny lining. This proved to be not only a revolution but a serious hazard. At that time I worked at a textile weaving factory (Grouts) in Gt. Yarmouth, half way down St. Nicholas Road where Sainsbury's now stands (St Nicholas Road, Great Yarmouth, Norfolk NR30 1NN). Working two shifts, 6 a.m. to 2 p.m. or 2 p.m. to 10 p.m. (when I was 18 it became "nights" as well) in this really noisy environment with the deafening sound of a thousand Looms clattering non-stop.

My job was a Battery Filler then; filling the Shuttles with new bails of thread and placing them in the "Battery" of shuttles to keep the looms running. Most of my 600 or so colleagues or workmates were almost *all* leather clad Rockers, like I was, or used to be. Imagine the reception I got when I turned up for work one sunny afternoon in the late summer of 63 wearing a pair of slick two-tone blue trousers and this collarless Beatle jacket. Even as I walked in the gate one of my "workmates" came up beside me and whilst supposedly inspecting the material slipped a lighted roll-up end into my left pocket. A minute later the smell of smouldering foam lining alerted me to the fact that I was on fire. One of my work mates shouting, "Do you smoke?" to which I hastily replied "Only when some twat drops a dog-end in my pocket!"

During that day, week, month and following six months I had more people threatening to beat me up than I can possibly recall. When I got cheesed off with the threats, I'd call them out, but none of them wanted to put their money where their mouth was and step out to settle it once and for all. We all had to carry a Sheath Knife, for work. That was used to cut the spare Warp off the Looms (if you were a Battery Filler) and cutting thread or cloth in other circumstances. If there had of been a fight and someone went for a knife, it could have got very messy. Gradually they got bored and accepted me or ignored me. Some remained friends and others shunned me because I looked different. Qué Sera Sera ("Whatever will be, will be." Spanish). I was just 16 then. I had left Great Yarmouth College of Arts & Crafts because I didn't want to progress on to either London or Manchester Art colleges. The thought of earning good money in factory shifts would serve me much better. It didn't! The money just goes. Nobody said that I could save and buy a new house for a few hundred quid when I was 18, or buy a car, go on holiday. Nobody told me I could invest my hard earned money, so I spent it instead. Such a waste. Life could have been so much different. Who knows?

Hey Joe!

There was also the Regent Bowl. I was working most of the time, and in my spare time I'd spend money on my mates who were worse off, treating them to coffee and snacks. The Bowling Alley, "Regent Bowl" a really good Juke Box in the glass-fronted bar that looked across the lanes and had a good snack bar too. Here the lovely Linda used to serve me and my pals with copious cups of coffee or tea, sandwiches and all as we chattered about or week. It was here in the mid-sixties that me and my good mate, Joe Cuttajar, serenaded a bevy of girls who gathered on several occasions to hear our renditions of "She Loves You", or of 'From A Jack to A King', covered by Jim Reeves not long before that.

> *(Chorus :)*
> *"From a jack to a king*
> *From loneliness to a wedding ring*
> *I played an ace and I won a queen*
> *And walked away with your heart."*

Joe was a great pal and we were a team. As he was a handsome dark-skinned and Mediterranean Maltese lad, the girls went mad for him. His summer job was working as a Change Giver at the first amusement arcade on the Promenade. He used to attract the girls like crazy. At one time he used to say, "Hey, don't worry. I arrange the girls for Saturday night, just meet me at 6 p.m. near the market place bust stop." When I turned up he told me, "The girls they came in to the amusement place all day (Majestic) and talk to me. I have two lined up for 6.15 by the ABC and if you don't like yours we have another two at 6.30 waiting by the Regent Bowl. If they are no good, then there are two more at the Britannia Pier at 6.45... oh, and two more by the Jetty at 7 o'clock." When I picked my lower jaw up off the pavement and asked jokingly if that was enough, he replied, "On no worries, there are two more by the Winter Gardens at 7.15 and two others by the Wellington Pier at 7.30!"

After picking my lower jaw up off the floor, my next question was, "What if we choose to go out with two of the earlier ones Joe, how are we going to dodge the others all night?" Gt. Yarmouth was not that big a place and being dark skinned he was not difficult to spot in a crowd! Bless him. We had some great times and good laughs that year. I spoke to Joe last year as I found him through a relative on Facebook and he phoned me up, all the way from Malta. It was great to speak to him again. He's now running Tourist Jeep trips on Gozo, near Malta. Joe didn't recall the Bowling Alley, but he did recall us two strolling up Regent Road, a guitar each, and playing some Beatles songs like "She Loves You" that we used to Duo on. That was just pure innocent fun and Joe was a good pal and all round good apple, as they say. His ability to pull girls, who I must add were *very* eager to be pulled by him, was just incredible. Made me wish I was darker skinned sometimes as I really struggled and was never any good at chatting-up women! I think we serenaded and dated two or three new girls each week. Nothing much ever came of these liaisons, but we did meet some interesting girls from far-off exotic places with names like Ilkley, Derby and Huddersfield. Thankfully we never bumped into any of the "extras" Joe had arranged to meet. They probably went off in a huff and quickly found some other holiday romance, as many were hoping for, when they set out for Great Yarmouth.

The irony of all that boy meets girl stuff was of course that at that age, 16, we had no idea about relationships and most teens were just rampant and bursting with "lurve" hormones. In seaside towns they come and they go, then after their holiday fling they go home, get a boring job and marry their boring boyfriends and settle down to the usual boring routine and shelling out kids; not because they want them, but their hormones are raging. Who'd be a teenager, eh? Let me be honest, if you got to kiss a girl then that was a hot date! If she let you touch her, and she undid your trousers and had a little play, then you'd say you just had sex! Teenagers were amazingly repressed and ignorant in those days. Having said that, they seem to *think* they know all about it nowadays but are just as clueless about relationships as we were then.

There were a few young women I met that were rather special... or was that just the hormones? One girl I recall had the surname 'Pimm' and said she was a member of the famous drinks family, but I don't think she was: that was just her excuse to try a Pimms on the Rocks later. These were mainly friendships, learning to be with the opposite sex and develop those friendships. As many times as we got fruity we got slapped back, though occasionally you'd meet a girl who was feeling horny, but as young lads we had little idea what to do! Like I said, I was still a virgin up to about 17, so these were all awkward and confusing lessons.

Then there was my friend Jackie. I was never sure if she fancied me or not. We'd often meet near the Brit, and just sit on the beach and chat, or cuddle up, like you see us here in the this picture. If my hand strayed from her waist, even accidentally, I'd get a sharp elbow nudge! She was a very attractive young woman and we did have some good times just talking: but when a teenage boy and hormones are rampant, talking is often the last thing on your mind. Often wonder what became of Jackie. I'll tell you ladies, it's not much fun being a "thick" young bloke, never understanding what is going on with you girls and usually missing out to some "wise guy" (as the Yanks call them) who had all the chat and the dance moves: though usually they turned out to be the least reliable husbands as they liked the chase! But there again I have heard so many stories of women marrying "ordinary safe men" but then doing the dirty on them because they wanted or lacked "excitement". That is such a

wrong thing to do. Men do it too, marry someone dull and plain woman then carry on behind their backs. This made me cautious about relationships at a very early age, that and the constant threats of STD's, which were frequent in those times and quite enough to scare good lads like me. We were bombarded with choices, but also well warned (by teachers who were ex-navy/army/etc.) but had little guidance outside of that. Heady times growing up.

There is me in the earliest of early Mod fashions, which was really a throw-back from 50's USA. The fashion was the Tee-shirt, with Iron-on lettering, a Crew Cut hairstyle and either American jeans or modern trousers (as I am in the above photo, c.1963. The lovely Jackie was looking very smart in her Mod Cheque suit with a natural hairstyle. I was probably wearing one of the early Timex watches: had a few of those as sand off the beach easily got in and messed up the works!

Mostly those days consisted of hanging out on the beach, in summer, or in town just mooching around until you met up with some pals. If you had the money you could of course go to a coffee bar, but that became expensive, especially as the owners didn't like anyone hanging around too long. One venue was Palmers 'Kenya Bar', secreted away upstairs. They had bamboo poles going up from artificial flower-boxes at the back of the shelved seating area, with stools (quite "trendy"). The whole area was decorated with what was supposed to look like tropical plants and vines, but all made of the latest plastic! I nearly set fire to the decor one day whilst trying to adjust the flame on my new refillable cigarette lighter. A flame shot up about three feet high amongst the tropical plastic leaves!

THE SMALL MACHINE WITH THE BIG PERFORMANCE

BSA BANTAM

everybody's motor cycle all over the world

MOTORBIKIN'

Like most lads of the time, before I turned Mod, I had my heart set on getting a motorbike. You had to be 17 before you could get any kind of two-wheeled vehicle. It had have a smaller engine at first, up to 250 c.c. I think, but there were not many that were 200 c.c. let alone 250 c.c. or even 125 c.c., so I had my eyes on a BSA Bantam. The Bantam of the mid-sixties was a sleek little thing, sometimes with an optional double seat, offering pillion space for your mates with a Full

Licence or later girlfriends. Although not hugely powerful, sporting a 125 c.c. to 175 c.c. engine, these were nippy little bikes and great fun to own; so my older mates told me.

My father was a very highly respected High Class Motor Engineer. He was the first person to deliver an Automobile (Car) into Great Yarmouth (a large white one for a local Doctor) in his adult years but was also a keen biker. Those days they used to ride chain-driven Rudge, or similar, and race them around the countryside, including through ponds and fields, in a race to get back first. He told me several of the more "tame" stories that you could tell your growing son, but carefully left out the more dangerous adventures for fear that I would emulate him.

(Left) This is my father on his Rudge motorcycle, c.1934 - roughly in his mid-twenties.

One story was that he and five or so pals were doing a cross-country, road, track, field and trail around Norfolk's then quiet lanes. My father had left two bikers behind, but had no idea where the others were, that is until he saw one hanging off a road sign, the pointy things that direct you to villages. He thought his mate had been impaled and was dead, as he hung there lifeless with the pointed sign appearing to stick through his body. He stopped in shock by the sign, gaping at his mate. Suddenly his mate lifted his head. "Are you seriously hurt?" enquired my father. "No Syd. Bloody bike catapulted me and this has gone through my jacket, but I'm not hurt, just ruddy stuck!" My father then realized that this man may have been near the leader. "Were you in third place?" "No." Came the reply. "I was second and going to flaming fast round that bend trying to catch Jack." (not his real name). Realizing that the tail-enders would get him down, my father suddenly saw a chance for victory. My father asked if he wanted a hand to get down. The man told him he was alright and my father should go quickly and catch-up with the leaders! "Hell, as long as you are all right, I could catch Billy!" The man waved him off. "Not a problem old man. Go on, be quick." He sped off. One of the "no chance to win" tail-enders helped the man down.

During the war my father had an Ariel Square Four. These were huge machines compared to the earlier motorcycles and had four cylinders instead of one or two. By that time he worked for Pertwee & Back, a motor vehicle dealer and repairer and was Foreman there. His skills with mechanical things were highly prized and when WWII broke out he wanted to become an Engine Room Artificer in the Navy. They would not have him as he was too short! He stayed at P&B and was often called out to help the war effort though, by the Navy! On one occasion a huge German Parachute Mine landed on South Denes and failed to go off. The Army called dad and said they were too busy to go defuse the thing, and could he and "the chaps" (his mechanics) take out the Breakdown Truck and tow it away somewhere (a naval yard?) There they were with a live "Luftmine A" (LMA) that was 500 kg (1,100 lb) and 5 ft 8 in (1.73 m) in length swinging from the tackle at the back of the truck. As one man drove, very, very slowly, the other three would walk with hands on the mine to try to stop it hitting anything and detonating. It's worth mentioning here that the Luftmine A was capable of flattening a factory, two rows of houses for roughly 100 yards or killing one-hundred people!

This is a picture (above left) of a Luftmine, but this one, in Scotland, was defused and disarmed before they moved it. As far as I know, nobody from my Dad's crew took pictures, they just moved the *live* mine and then went back home for some sleep!

At many other times the Navy called him. Great Yarmouth harbour could be easily blocked if just one ship was sunk in the entrance, so the navy tended to use Lowestoft for quick repairs or short refuelling calls. My father was called out many times to repair Motor Torpedo Boats (MTB) or Minesweepers that were busy defending the channel. First he had to go to Gt. Yarmouth's southernmost Fishwharfe where he'd collect spares from the Navy stores. Whilst there he discovered that they stocked "redundant" piston rings that would fit his Ariel Square Four. With permission, he took some of these, gasket cork and filled his tank with High Octane fuel. He had worked out that he could get to Lowestoft in less than half the time and so get the boats back out to sea more efficiently. In one of his many tales, he told me that he made it from Fishwharfe to Lowestoft harbour in just over four minutes, which, he quietly added, "that was not bad as there was an air raid on at the time…" He explained that the roads were full of potholes and even unexploded bombs here and there, plus he could not use any lights (they were often night time trips.) Still he made it in just a few minutes! As cool as a cucumber my Dad.

It was for these reasons and many more like them that my Dad refused to let me own a motorbike. In one of his rare moments, other than letting me just get on with it, he sat me down one day and told me why, adding "I was a mad bastard and I know you would be too. To tell you the truth I don't want to see my only son, who I love, killed on a bloody motorbike!" It came as a shock, but was good, in a way. I respected my Dad a lot more for that bit of honesty and of course showing that he cared: not something that many men of that era did with their kids as they'd come through a harsh war and were brought up in hard ways, taught just top shut-up and get on with it.

(Left) This was my father and mother, Sydney James and Ivy Symonds, at the reopening of E.C.M.E.C. Garage, c.1961 when they became official Volkswagen Dealers. He was the M.D. Had all the ideas, did all the hard work and got little thanks from Burrell's Engineering. (E.C.M.E.C. stood for East Coast Motor Engineering Company.)

The garage was visited one day by a mysterious German man who just wandered in and looked around. My father was in the garage at the time and greeted him. He introduced himself as a Site Manager for Volkswagen ("Folk's vagen") from Hanover in Germany. My father was curious as he had worked on German equipment during WWII and thought their engineering to be quite worthy; different story nowadays! The man said that they were looking to have a VW Dealership in Great Yarmouth and thought that E.C.M.E.C.

Might be the best place for it. My father then had words with Edgar Burrell who was persuaded. The garage was stripped and rebuilt with no delays and no messing around. Efficiency.

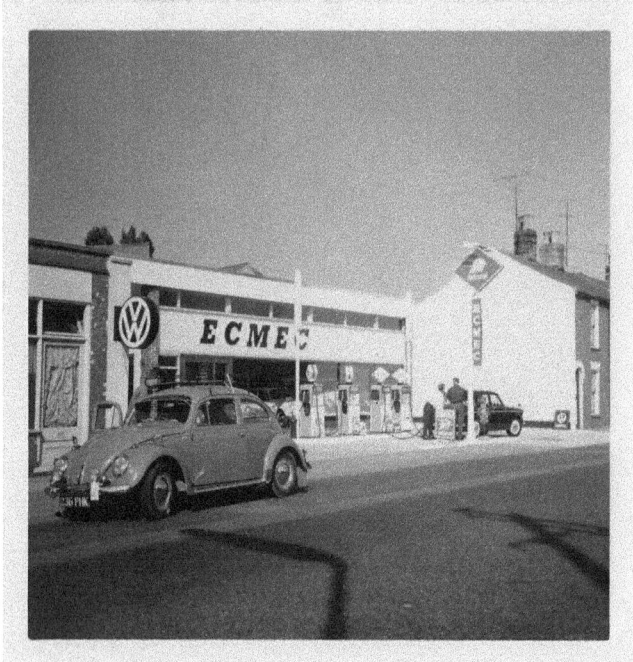

In this picture, taken by my Dad with an Agfa Isola 120 mm Camera, you see the garage just after it reopened as a VW Dealership, c.1961. These were the days when there was a small cylinder next to the petrol pumps which contained Two Stroke Oil; about 1d per pump! There would be a similar one with Red-X in. This was and still is used to keep your engine clean and free from carbon build-ups, etcetera. Nothing like that exists for Scooters though and I'm not sure if the original can be used with Two-Stroke.

However, it was just before the garage was modernised that I recall there being two small Scooter-Skis in the Showroom. I must have been about 14 then. These were probably among the first powered "jet skis", as they called now, and were very Vespa-like in appearance. Whether they were made by Vespa or not I cannot recall. Perhaps sitting on these machines and imagining that I was whizzing over the waves influenced my decision to become a Mod?

Not far down the line I saw some Scooters around, not many and mainly old men going to work on them. Then I'd see a glimpse of some teenager with long hair (gasp!) riding a scooter and smiling, but there were only a couple in GY at that time and they were not particularly Mods. The fashions were a bit slow to come to town. Having been refused a motorcycle and being a fan of the "new scene", these scooters looked like fun. The Vespa (one of which is pictured here) was an attractive machine, but in particular I liked the Lambretta. Girls in Italy used to ride side-saddle a lot, this was usually for two reasons;

1. They preserved their modesty whilst wearing skirts and 2. They counter-weighted the Vespa's off-balance engine by dangling their legs over the left side (although in this picture the lady has her legs on the right side, for some reason).

You used to see many Vespa's with scraped side panels on the "off-side" where the rider had a close encounter with gravity, the right-sided engine often throwing it over in a skid. Having been brought up with an engineer of practical abilities I saw no point in having an unbalanced machine. Being the star he was my father bought me a Lambretta. He also told me that it was "safer than a motorcycle" and had leg shields that offered some protection. Somehow though I think he'd forgotten what he said before, you know, about being "a mad bastard" and that I'd be like him too!

There may be a few people who have different views of the above statements, but that's alright. We all get told different things by others who perceive things in their own way. That is life. Variety and unpredictability.

Many older men were using Motor Scooters as a means of transport to and from work. Birds Eye Foods in Gt. Yarmouth had its own scooter club. All "respectable gentlemen" in correct attire and usually with windscreens on the front that were bigger than the scooter! Of course, they frowned upon teenagers getting scooters, riding them fast or tarting them up to look nice: "Why, it's just not proper old chap! And as for this sort of behaviour... well... it's just not on!"

One of the very best things about owning a "Motor Scooter" is that they can be customised add-infinitum. Just the options of paintwork alone are phenomenal, let alone what can be written on it, then custom accessories, etc. Individual expression was born in the 60's and we said a very hearty goodbye to the Henry Ford principle: you can have any colour you like as long as it's black!

(When I first saw this picture I thought it was Batman's sidekick taking a break!)

1963 also saw the biggest changes on the music scene since Bill Haley and The Comets rocked around the clock in America. Bill Haley was the man, with a "kiss curl" who got teenagers raving to rock-and-roll music, much to the disgust of parents of the time. The music was punchy, fast and featured these new things called "electric guitars" that made even louder noises than the drums that were being beaten like crazy! That was in the late 1950's, so by 1963 things were starting to Rock in the UK too. But we did have some unusual acts coming to the surface too. These were the years when things were opening up, horizons broadened and young people wanted to experiment. We saw the unforgettable Lonnie Donnigan and his "Skiffle" band playing fun music, like "My Old Man's a Dustman". There were wandering minstrels in the streets with acoustic guitars, singing as they wandered, like me and Joe did, but these guys all had long "mop-style" hair and wore Duffle Coats. There were called Beatniks. Remember them? Yes? Wow, you're old! :-D (See, to hell with convention!) Music started to diversify and in USA there were new types of music forming from a melting pot of Folk, Country, Rock and Pop. Those people we'd sent away from Great Britain, in rickety wooden boats, had eventually done something worthwhile then!

We had Juke Boxes in Pubs, clubs and Cafés. Many songs were love songs, some tragic, like "Tell Laura I love Her", others just soppy or romantic. The Beatles were a new breed of musician. At first they didn't have much mastery of their guitars (about three or four chords, which is about average, to be fair) but they just had that magic knack of creating a new tune, lyrics that were fresh and that many teenagers could easily relate to. Simple things like "Love, love me do. You know I love you." and "I'll get you in the end." Oh yeah... that reminds me of a girl I'd met, on holiday in GY, and she used to hold me tight, kiss me and sing it to me, also giving a subtle reference towards my trousers as she sang "get you in the end"! Ha ha ha, the memories that come back.

Liverpool seemed to be the epicentre of the new music eruption and, oh boy, were we glad about that. In fact we were "Glad all over!" (Ho ho ho!) 1963 was the beginning of a world-changing era that we were in at the very heart of. I have heard many of my pals say the same thing, "we were so lucky to have been there" and it's so very true. Sometimes, when I see the teenagers of today, locked into their mobile phones, play stations and other electronic rubbish, I actually feel very sorry for them. They have nothing, but we had it all. They could have it all today, but only if they get up off their lazy arses and get out there and make it happen.

1963. That is the year when teenagers made the most of work, sunshine and transport and went out and had fun. We made it happen, lived life to the full when possible and made use of every hour of our time that we were not working. Thank heavens we didn't have the Internet or Mobile Phones then! We had to talk to real people, buy real records and you saw real musicians in the local Pubs, Clubs and Theatres.

The Charts in 1963 featured:
Gerry and the Pacemakers - You'll never Walk Alone.
The Beatles - She Loves You
The Searchers - Sugar and Spice
Roy Orbison - Blue Bayou/Mean Woman Blues
Cliff Richard - Don't Talk To Him
Brian Pool and The Tremelos - Do You Love Me?
Shirley Bassey - I (who have nothing)
Crystals - Then He Kissed Me
Billy J Kramer & the Dakotas - I'll Keep You Satisfied

Trini Loppez - If I Had a Hammer
Adam Faith - The First Time
Peter, Paul & Mary - Blowing In The Wind
Elvis Presley - Bossa Nova Baby.

Just from that excerpt, you can see the wide variety. Compare that with the mind-numbing elctro-drivel and C-Rap that pours out across the board nowadays! Is it any wonder that many new performers now are trying to go back to the solo guitarist or Pop group type line-up? Not at all.

The Mod fashions became popular. My electric-blue two-tone trousers were a hit with me. I can even remember walking back from the Pleasure Beach one day, feeling good. Two girls walked past the other way and said "Wow, look at those trousers!", *not* "Wow, look at hat cool young man!", which would have made me feel better. Ha ha ha! But seriously, you could feel the buzz in the air - alright, maybe some of it was just teenage excitement, but that certainly contributed to the general feel of the times. We knew something was happening, little did any of us realise just what, or how big it would be.

In '63 the evenings were mainly spent walking about with mates, or just sitting around chatting GY was one of those places where your mates knew lots of other people, so you'd get introduced and before you know it, you know lots and lots of people. Weekends were "up the town" (do we say this for the same reason as "High Street"?), sitting around in various coffee bars and looking for someone to hang-out with. Too much coffee was really bad as you wanted to go for a pee every ten minutes and the excess caffeine dose made me speak like a robot with a bad electrical connection stuck on high speed! Mind you, in later life that early "caffeine abuse" can give you some understanding about why there's so much tension in USA and other big coffee swilling countries!

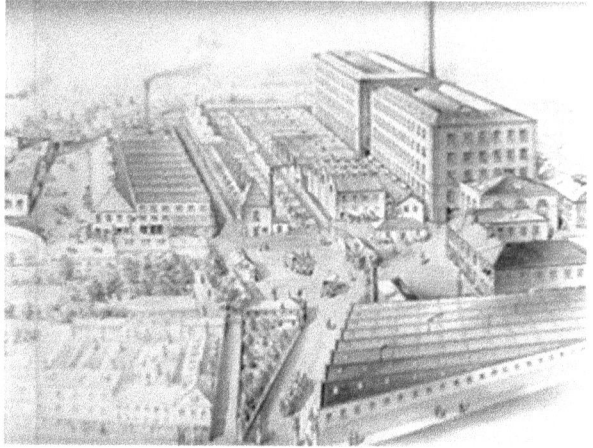

The 'Fab Four' certainly take a lot of the credit for changing our lifestyles and outlooks. They were the first Mod style band and others followed. Incidentally, I heard that when they stayed at the Carleton Hotel in 1963 they made quite a mess of their rooms. Was it them who started that trend amongst bands too?

Winter Nights.
Oh they were dull, cold and dreary! Long dark nights and dark clouds too, all combined with Easterly winds that were said to be "Lazy winds": they were too lazy to go around you, so went through you. Chilled to the bone as you walked along the almost deserted seafront. All of the cafes, amusements and other businesses all boarded up. Many of the owners gone to sunnier climbs or curled up indoors by a roaring fire. It was too cold to go out unless you needed to.

Going to work in such dismal conditions was even less fun. Especially working the early shift (6 a.m. to 2 p.m. For those who never knew what Shifts were; lucky sods!) The Double-Decker Buses, most people's only option to get to work, were packed. Upstairs was where smoking was allowed. Normally you could get just one or two seats there, downstairs was packed and less polluted. The smoke you could cut out with a knife and take away with you, it was that thick! Not the best start to the morning.

In '63 I was still at Grouts (pictured opposite - unknown artist's impression) working two shifts; 6-2 & 2-10. They said that when I was 18 that I would have to work three shifts, so including the dreaded nights - 10-6. This I tried to dodge by getting a day job in another department. That was where that idiot Ernie tried winding me up.

The next year, 1964 was to be all change, 17 and old enough to drive a small motorbike or scooter. As stated elsewhere in this book, my father had already decided that fate for me.

Where the scooter was bought from I'm not sure, but it may have been Newtown Motors, one of my father's old pals in the trade. He chose it for me, with my agreement; as he knew good from bad lots. Anyway, I came home from work one day and there it was, waiting in the garage for me. All I had to do was get 'L' Plates and insurance, and I was ready to go. Having ridden a push-bike all I needed was to get familiar with the clutch and gears; a three speed affair and very simple.

 It was a 1958 Lambretta Ldb 150 Mk3. The newer Li model, would have been about £132 new then. Factory colour of the LD was a mid-tone Blue with cream contrast. It was then over five years old so not in bad condition at all, no rust and a good runner. If I remember rightly the price was about £30; or should I say £30. 00s. 00d (for those who do not know, the currency then was Pounds, Shillings and Pence but the pence

sign was a "d", making it Lsd and not to be confused with 'Lysergic diethylamide' or 'acid' the hallucinogenic drug!) My Dad, bless him, chose it for me and I think that he was pleased that I followed his wishes and would have some metal faring around me for protection. Not that it protected you from everything, especially accidents, as they would happen often enough on 8" wheels!

(For any readers who do not know of wheel sizes, this is the diameter of the metal part of the wheel, the Hub and Rim, around which the Tyres go. The 8" wheels and tyres were not much bigger than what you'd see on a Wheelbarrow! Later Lambretta moved up to 10" wheels which were marginally safer.) Marginally. You can add between 3" and 4" for tyre width, so bringing them up to a minimum of around (ha ha "a round" get it?!) 11" on the 8" wheels. Still not exactly made for cornering at speeds.

Getting used to the new transport was easy as I used it for work; much nicer than those smokey old busses! Work ranged from Grouts Textile Factory to Lacons Brewery and later bouncing between Birds Eye and Lacons, eventually settling at Birds eye Foods for the longer term.

While I was at Lacons, I started on the Empty Bottle floor where Geoff and me kept six young women supplied with empties that had to be rinsed and cleaned. They sat three either side of a kind of "chain washer", this having spouts that the bottles were put over, the machine then blasting them with a water and cleaning solution. Labels were also washed off in the following process. Then the bottles would be warmed - to avoid cracking - and rinsed again with hot steam to kill any bacteria. I worked there in the early 60's up in the Empties Department (just hidden behind the tree) with Geoff Lingwood and his father

Jack; well know for riding his racing bike from Caister every day. We had a few laughs up there, especially as the six girls who worked with us were always up for a laugh. One of them was trying to physically get me off-balance one day, so I spun her around and held her arms behind her back, "Now I've got you!"" I said optimistically. Almost without hesitation she pushed back and used both hands to grab my tackle; but only squeezed gently, thank heavens! They were feisty women in those days.

After that department got a bit boring I moved down to the Bottling Floor. This was kind of in the middle of the factory, behind the Empties and just back from the Brewing floor. Here freshly filled bottles rattled and rolled along roller belts towards Homogenisers; large machines which steamed the bottles to again kill any bacteria. They would then go through a labelling machine. Part of my job was to keep the labelling girls fed with stacks of the correct labels; e.g. Brown Ale, Pale Ale, Barley Wine, etc. These all had to be checked and were then marked via a series of little nicks along the edge of the label, telling the date and batch. Glue also had to be kept topped up as labels can't stick without it. That was someone else's job though. Mine was keep the girls supplied, watch out for and clear any blockages and also try to stop any bottles or crates of bottles falling off the line. One did one one day while I was clearing another. One bottle exploded as it hit the floor and I saw a glint of a small shard of glass heading for my eye, so deftly held my palm up! The shard entered my palm instead of my eye, thankfully.

Here's some Gt Yarmouth history! Memory: Lacons Brewery. This photo was taken around the mid-sixties, by the looks of the Hillman Minx parked up on Brewery Plain. Those two schoolboys, from the Priory School, could have been myself and one of my classmates from some time earlier. After school, if I was lucky enough to have the bus fare sometimes, I would jump on the N. 1 or No. 2 bus home.

After the bottling floor I left and went to Birds Eye. Can't recall my first job there, but it wasn't very exciting. On asking if I could do something better the Supervisor told me they needed Fork Truck Drivers, but I'd have to apply and then take my driving test on one. That I did. Easy pass. That came in handy for later when I went back there.

At one point I went back to Lacons and worked in the Stores, mainly loading the barrels of fresh ales onto pallets as they rolled down the tunnel under the back street; it was a "downhill site" so they made use of it. That may have been between the Bottling Floor and the return to Birds Eye, I'm not 100% sure. One summer I spent back at Lacons on the Drays. What an excellent job! Starting of on local rounds, you'd help the Drayman (Driver) to load up the Dray according to which stops were first or last. My sense of humour has always been quite dry, so the Drayman didn't always get it if I asked about the Pub in Caister, "Is the First & Last first or last today?"

My scooter served me well for getting to work in 1964 and was totally reliable. As there were barely any Mods in Great Yarmouth during the early part of that year, there were no similarly minded pals to go riding with. None of my pals at that time had a scooter, or even a motorcycle at that time either. In fact Greg Long was the first "biker" of any sort that I met! In Great Yarmouth the scooter scene really didn't take off until late '64 or early '65. It was pretty lonely until then!

Overall, not much happened at all on the Mod front of things, at least in Great Yarmouth. The USA fashions; Crew Cut, Tee Shirt with iron-on tape own designs and two-tone trousers. I was one of the first, if not the first to change fashion and later get a scooter. Little did I know what adventures this would all lead to during 1964, 65 and 66!

Make yourself a cuppa and get comfortable, ready for the adventures - at least the ones that can be safely printed, the mishaps, teenage cock-ups and more historic trivia.

Profit margins on books are very low, but they do cost a lot to set-up and print. So, if you like it please leave a review on the bookseller's website as this helps; the more good reviews and likes the easier it is found amongst the millions of others!

Chapter 2.

1964: BECOMING MORE MOD.

It was big "Hooray!" when I turned 17 in January 1964. I suppose, by nature, I was always "modern", but never realized it at the time. If you are still thinking about that, we are all where we are "now" and are therefore by definition "modern" or up to date. Becoming Mod in a fashion sense was quite different though as one really did not have to think about it. You have money, you go out, you buy the clothes that you like and other people label you "Mod". No big deal, that is until someone takes an instant dislike to you and decides to persecute you, just because you are different and growing up in an experimental society. That's what the police did, all over the country. At first they persecuted the "Ton-up Boys" on their Motorcycles. Then they went after Mods, because we were different and they didn't understand us wanting to have fun and adventures. Someone in London, around 1962/3 apparently, started the trend for Italian scooters and fashions by offering custom parts for the bikes. We didn't know about that at the time, that was just a London thing. Like most of the crap going on about Mods, Londoners said the most, claimed the most and bragged the most. At the blunt end in G.Y. we knew little about what went on in London and Brighton, or really cared come to that. That was all hype, much of it caused or created by the Press; mostly based in London, of course; it seems that anything not based in London has to justify itself. Competition, I suppose. The Press, or "shite hawks" as they were known, used to blow any story about Mods and fights out of all proportions, just to make headlines. Of course, this had a ripple effect with the gullible public who believed that they were all going to get beaten up or murdered by "rampaging armies of Mods"! Unlike the Press that we know and love, surely?! However, having said all that, the odd few of us did see stories about "Mod Invasions" in the rags and were quite excited by it... not at the thought of riots, just being part of such a burgeoning group of younger people who were having fun.

1964 saw "The Battle of Hastings"... according to the Press. A few Mods had a clash with a few Rockers and of course the shite-hawks had a field day. From there on in they saw it as fair game to persecute Mods or Rockers as "wild youths" and "out of control" and any other drivel their mucky warped minds could conjure up.

Clacton too saw its first gatherings of the Mods: just look at the picture left to see how they rioted! Disgraceful! "Ho ho ho." What makes me laugh about this group of possibly London Mods, is the mickey-take hats: almost all businessmen in Londinium would wear a Bowler hat to show that they worked in the city, so many Mods adopted similar hats as a symbol that they could wear what they liked and did not conform. The hats know as Pork Pie Hats became very popular. People in the background or passing by would stop and stare, after all, this was a new and completely irregular event, these youths wearing smart casual clothes under a scruffy used American war coat. Oh the shock of it all. By the way, I like the "posh" scooterist with the suitcase on the back instead of a rucksack or sleeping bag!

Side-Swiped.

It was after I had owned the scooter for a while that things started to happen. Around about the beginning of April 1964, on a Saturday night, I went over to Gorleston-on-Sea and looked for anyone to hang out with. The streets were pretty quiet then and not many youngsters had any form of transport, other than "push bikes". Eventually I met a young man called Greg Long who was riding a BSA Bantam 125cc motorcycle. He was parked outside a coffee bar in Gorleston, The Chalet Coffee Bar, chatting to a couple of young girls who were "scouting" and then invited us all to a 18th(?) Birthday party at their house, just on the Bridge. Greg knew the way so I followed him. It was a big house just on the entrance to the bridge that leads to Gorleston Cliffs; what we used to call "the posh end". Opposite the bridge now stands the James Paget Hospital; something that I had a hand in building later on, 1978-79. We arrived the house and saw only a small gathering. The girl who lived there was blonde and, I think, had just turned 18 so having what she called a party. To be honest, I've seen more exciting parties in a graveyard. It was quiet, very quiet. Mum and Dad were there too so no loud music or dancing was allowed. Some modern Pop songs were being played at a very moderate level, like parents would listen to the news at, just audible! Soft drinks were being served in glasses with strict instructions not to wander around with them or spill any on the luxury pile carpets.

At one stage I recall someone saying "Here, come and look at this!" in tone of disbelief. We followed him to the family bathroom upstairs whereupon we were shown a new low style toilet suite with another odd looking thing beside it. Someone asked why they had two toilets. The girl said "No, silly, it's a Bidet!" Me, I had no idea, so just kept quiet and listened. "A bee what?" asked another. "It's for washing your bottom after going to the toilet" explained the girl's sister. Of course, someone had to pipe up "Errr, that's disgusting! What's wrong with toilet paper?" The whole thing was rather boring after that so we wandered back outside.

Greg and his mate said they knew where a better party might be and asked me if I wanted to go. It was apparently the other side of the Magdalene Estate. As I was no wiser, Greg said "Follow me Mick. I know the way." (Most people called me "Mick" then.) Off he went onto the estate, along Brasenose Avenue, and within a little way started to open up the Bantam and speed off in front of me. Still being a novice rider wit 'L Plates' up, I was not that cock sure of the bike like Greg was with his Bantam, so did my best to follow. Not far along Brasenose Avenue I saw Greg pass a junction. As I approached the same junction - possibly Granta Way - I saw a car's headlights coming towards the main road from the side street. I could just see glimpses of headlights across the garden walls and through the shrubs. We met at the junction. As you know if you have ever ridden a scooter or motorbike, you cannot make sudden moves or brake hard as it could prove fatal. As it happens, the driver of the car could not brake hard either. The bloody idiot shot straight out and side-swiped me! The impact was his bumper hitting my scooter side on. It's an odd feeling, going straight and then suddenly being shunted sideways, like a Red Ball slammed into the middle pocket. The scooter flipped onto its left side and ended up across the road just into the junction on the other side. It was literally knocked out from under me. As he overshot the junction, and I was thrown off after travelling sideways with the scooter for a good yard or three. Just as well the roads were not too busy in those days. Today you would be thrown into the path of an oncoming truck, bus or car from one or possibly even two directions; e.g. the opposite side road too! Greg was completely unaware of the accident as he was by then already around a hundred yards ahead of me and accelerating. I was shaken up and had injuries to my left leg and arm, bad bruising on my hip, etcetera. The car driver said he didn't see me: the truth is the idiot didn't slow down or even look.

When I saw Greg a week or two later he said that the party was non-existent anyway and that his mate had got it wrong. My body was bruised and my mind shaken. Little did I realise that by the time I sat to write this book I would have experienced just about every kind of physical and mental trauma there is! Every time after that shocking event that I saw a car coming from the side roads it used make me very nervous. Even now, whether on the scooter or in my car, if I see someone approaching a left junction at speed I tend to feel a bit edgy. My scooter fared better than me though as my good old Dad took it into the garage, straightened it out and made it safe to ride again. He was concerned for me and I think very glad that it wasn't a motorbike, as my leg would have been smashed to bits by the car's steel bumper. As it was I had a limp for a while, bad shoulder and possible a few fractures and you can't just pop into the local body shop and get those repaired like you can your scooter. It was a couple of weeks before the scooter was repaired and I could get back on it. It needed a bit of paint too, so I decided to paint it up myself. There was no such thing as spray cans in those days, not for the commoners anyway. Dad's home garage was a god place to look. There I found a tin of what I'd call "French Blue" paint and some metallic silver too. Having asked my father if they were compatible, I set about painting the scooter, by hand, of course.

Within a couple of weeks I was almost healed and back on the road again. By this time there were a few other lads on scooters around Gt Yarmouth too. You know how it is, vague recollections only after fifty years, but recollections they still are. Early 1964 and there I was sitting on my scooter outside the new coffee bar at the bottom end of Regent Road. Just sit outside, waiting for anyone to come along who had a scooter. I waited, and waited. After a while, one day, I hear a roar of a scooter that sounded quite like mine. Suddenly this Lambretta LD shot along the seafront heading north. The rider's long wavy brown hair was billowing out behind him as he enjoyed his ride. I didn't meet him until later though. He, like me, was one of the first scooterists in town had an old Lambretta LD not too dissimilar to mine. It was not someone I knew at the time but later he became one of the frequent so-called "in-crowd", and that was a long-haired lad called "Churchie" or Brian Church to give a proper name. In late 2015 I caught up with him at the Chalet Coffee Bar in Gorleston; a place of homage now to those greater days. Over the past two or so years I have had some great reunions with old pals and they have jogged my memory. More about my memory, or lack of it, later.

Greg was a bit of a character. After passing his test on his BSA Bantam, he wanted a scooter. His Dad, being well off from the milk and bakery trade (Longs, on Englands Lane opposite The Chalet) bought him a brand new Lambretta GT200, plus a large shed and a complete set of Metric tools! It was the latter that made me laugh, but Greg's Dad knew he liked to tinker with engines, so the tools were part of the present. Greg was then left to get on with it. Greg rode the GT200 and decided that it was fast, but not quite fast enough. He decided to give the new machine) a bigger bore and skim the cylinder head a bit to get more speed from it. It almost worked. A triumphant Greg took the scooter out, opened it up and "bang!" blew the head off it! Time for a new engine. I did hear that Greg blew-up the second engine too. Not sure if that's true. He soon gave up scootering and bought sports cars instead. At that time I was working at Birds Eye Foods in Great Yarmouth, a place I worked at for many years of my life, or so it seemed. The scooter reliably got me to work and back in all weathers.

When it was raining you had to be very careful as the old busses used to leak diesel fuel all over the roads, with accumulated patches at bus stops or junctions. Cornering on eight inch wheels was bad enough in the dry, depending on the camber of the road, but in the wet, treacherous, especially on 8" wheels! The diesel patches became slippery like ice when it rained and it was easy to lose the back end as you cornered or braked, as I found out later on Beaconsfield Road. Returning home one evening I turned the corner from Nelson Road into Beaconsfield and saw this rear-end wheel sliding into view on the right side, as the bike tilted leftwards. There was a young woman standing on the Bus Stop, holding an umbrella. I had to let the bike go and just dive off the left side. The scooter skidded across the road and bounced of the far corner of Walpole Road, while I slid and hit the curb nearer to Nelson Road side! Slightly shaken, and more worried about my scooter, I sat up, rather shakily, as you do. I looked at my poor scooter laying on its side then looked across the road at the young woman on the Bust stop. Something inside my head half expected her to be concerned and maybe coming to help, but no, she just stood there trying to look as if she hadn't noticed. Weird. This prompted my sense of humour and I piped up "I'm not dead. Don't rush to call an ambulance or anything, I'm only injured!" Still she huddled under her brolly and tried to ignore me.

Work was one thing, but in the evenings and at weekend we wanted to go out and have fun, meet people, hang out in trendy places…. Well, as trendy as they got in Great Yarmouth. Acquiring this revolutionary marvel of transport was in late winter to early spring 1964: you had to be 17 to get a motorbike and Provisional Licence. There were hardly any other young scooterists on the road then. The first period of ownership was quite boring in terms of "pals" as none of my direct pals had one, so no "ride-outs", as they are known now, were possible. It was just a case of having some spare time, get on, ride around town and hope that you would bump into another scooterist: not literally, of course. The 'Big V' was opened in that spring or summer, but the early winter was a quiet as the grave in Gt Yarmouth.

Joseph Peter Vettese (Tribute)
A gentleman born in Scotland, but of fine Italian heritage, opened up a large Café at the end of Regent Road. That was Joseph Peter Vettese (Pron.

"Vet-tes-ay"). It had a large glass frontage, and side windows and a huge 'V' for Vettese on the front. It was their flagship Café.

Naturally, we all called it "The big V" as it had that huge 'V' for Vettese on the upper corner. It became a regular venue for many years, especially in the summer months. We may have been too young to appreciate it fully then, but looking back, "wow!" that was a really cool place to be.

(Left: Look what they've done to the Big V Ma!)

The coffee, ice cream and everything else they sold was excellent and generally they did not seem to mind how long we sat in there; contrary to many other places that hustled you out as soon as you finished your food or drink.

We also used to go to the Wimpy Bar (one such place that hustled youths out quickly), new Bowling Alley and of course any other place that would have us. Many café owners did not like crowds of youths making loud conversations and generally mingling, especially when most of them were "Boracic Lint" (skint) and could not afford to keep buying coffees, rolls or burgers. The Big V was terrific café with Italian coffee, teas, ice creams and a modern Juke Box too. As Mods liked Italian style so it was ideal.

One story from the Big V: We were sat at a table once just at the back of the stairs. The Juke Box played Dave Clark Five's

"Bits and pieces" with its heavy, thumping drum beat. We were, quite innocently, thumping on the table and singing along, as you do when in your teens. The biggest of the Vettese men appeared from the kitchen, it was oldest son Joseph (named after his father). He was about 6' 5" (six-foot five inches) tall and very angry. Glaring at us as he rolled his sleeves higher he growled "You boys thump-a on-a my table I work-a so hard to put in and I thump your heads together!" We stopped.

There was a woman called Phyllis who ran the Coffee Bar then. She used to mother me a bit, or was it "big sister" or something else? When I had a date, which was fairly frequent in those heady young days, she'd whisk me up a raw egg in milk with a couple of sugars and tell me to drink it down quickly, saying "That'll put lead in your pencil!" This I found rather strange, and didn't really equate a date with drawing, but complied and drank it down in one go: with a few mates giving it "Eww! How could you?" Then off I'd go on my date. Not much is remembered about girlfriends in those days as we met so many people it was hard to remember ones that you met only for a couple of days. As they say, like ships that pass in the night. It's a shame really, as we were so young and carefree, with our new mode of transport and instant friends everywhere, that I don't think we even thought about "permanent" or lasting friendships. We were all experimenting too. At the time I didn't realise, but a young lad called peter worked in the Big V. Peter Rouse, he, Brian Harden and me later became pals and used to hang out together, way into the 70's in fact and even after we all got married.

John Nockolds, another of the early GY 65 CLUB members and a great bloke to hang out with. He was part of the crowd who were more fun and spontaneous and liked to go for random ride-outs. One of John's "random rides" was actually at The Big

V, I was reminded. He and Chris Baker-Pretty were sitting outside on their scooters. Looking into the wide doorway, Chris noticed that the stairs were quite wide and had shallow steps. He dared John to ride his scooter up the stairs. With no more to do John revved his scooter up, rode to the top of the stairs and back down again! Nobody got hurt: John wouldn't have done it were that possible, but he did get a rollicking from the

Vettese's and barred. There were some of the boys you just shouldn't dare, and some who didn't need to be dared!

The Vettese's were a great family and sometime later I used to hang out with Alfredo Vettese, who taught me Ten Pin Bowling with a mate called Teddy Griffin. Teddy was only about 4' 6" tall and he chose the biggest, heaviest bowling ball that he could find, a 16 lb black ball. Unfortunately Teddy picked one with very small finger holes. He went to bowl, as Alfredo had shown us, arced the ball forwards and upwards, but his fingers were stuck tight, so the ball's weight and momentum took him up, off his feet and about three feet into the air. He landed on his back with a thud, the still stuck bowling ball landing on his stomach. He wasn't hurt, but Alfredo and me were in hysterics! That's a sight I'll never forget.

Great Yarmouth was very much alive in those days and people flocked to the place for their summer holidays. Seasonal jobs were so easy to find, in fact there were so many that most people had too much choice. One of the local crowd lads worked almost every establishment on Regent Road in just one week! There was a young fella, nicknamed "Peewee" who got himself a job in the Big V coffee bar, working with Phyllis and the others. He was too young for a scooter at the time, but did get one later and soon crashed on it. In 2013 I bumped into him again at a Scooter Rally in GY, and we both agreed that we'd get another scooter. He's got one now and is thoroughly enjoying it. Making up for lost time. One of Peewee's favourite sayings is "Procrastination is the thief of time." Go for it fella!

Fab is for Fabulous!

The Big V was always busy and we went in there quite a lot, especially at weekends. It was a place to meet friend, make new friends and for girls to go and "make themselves seen" in the hopes of meeting the boys they fancied. As stated earlier, I got know Alfredo Vettese and his brothers. I shall never forget Fabio. A very smartly dressed man, three-piece suits and Camel Hair overcoat draped over his shoulders. His black Italian hair slicked back with Brylcreem and wearing a Carnation in his button-hole he looked the archetypical handsome Italian male movie star. He, myself, Alfredo, Teddy Griffin and one of Alfie's other brothers (his name escapes me) were walking along the seafront one day. Some girls were walking toward us and spotted Fabio. As they approached, mouths hanging open at Fabio's looks, he held out a hand for any of them to grasp, and said "Hello. I'm Fabio. But you can call me Fab!" The girls just stood there still wide-eyed. We were hard pressed not to roll on the floor laughing!

Alfredo was at the other end of the spectrum, he just dressed plainly and casually and was very down-to-earth. Once you got to know the Vettese family they were just good hard working people who were trying to make a living. Even though rumours were floating around that they were linked to the Italian Mafia. Did we care? No. Was it true? Probably not. Friends were friends and we had some good times. Joseph Peter Vettese, the father and founder of the café scene in Great Yarmouth, to who we all owe a belated "Thank you!", died in November 2015. His beloved wife Luigina Notarianni, had gone before him. Of course Notarianni was a name that we all came to know later when Remo Notarianni opened his café in the Royal Arcade. Bless them all!

My Lambretta wasn't used all the time. In the summer there was just too many things to do and loads of fun to be had. To be honest, after four or five crashes, I'm amazed that I was still alive to enjoy it all! Micky Allen (Mick the Bomb) borrowed it once and smashed it up. He was very upset, but gladly not badly hurt. He had probably been showing off and the scooter ran away with him!

The picture here shows it in its last incarnation, after about my fifth accident, sporting a 6v VW Horn slung under the left leg shield, a VW Spotlight above it and a new Front Carrier (the same one Barry Pigano caught!). She was thing of beauty! This was after my father had souped it up. It became slightly faster than a TV 175

'Lucky' GY 59'ers.
1958 LDb 150 'BEX 325'

with a top speed around 75 mph and rapid acceleration.

Speaking of Micky....

Amusements.
There were many Amusement Arcades along the seafront. There was the 'Majestic', the one where my pal Joe had worked in 1963. Then there were the two long arcade ones, The Stagecoach Amusements – no, we never worked out why it was called that either but I think the owner may have been keen on Westerns!

In the arcade nearest to the Empire, they had a really good Jukebox at the back. Many of us would go in there on a Friday or weekend come 1964 to hear the latest Top Ten records. My mates used to call me "Mick" most of the time. We had another pal who was called "Mick the Bomb" (he always wore a 'Ban the Bomb' badge) and that was Micky Allen, then there were other pals, like Nick, Vicky Turner, Tony and Rick Elvin and many more. 'Mick The Bomb' Allen had a great idea one day. Our pals used to come in say something like "Hello Mick, Mick. Have you seen Vick?" So Micky thought it a good idea to give everybody numbers. He called me Mick 1, himself Mick 2, and so on. So when one of the lads came in and said "Hello Mick 1, Mick 2. Have you seen Nick 5 or Vick 1?" we would know exactly who they were referring to! We ended up with around 14 Micks, 7 Nicks, 4 or 5 Dicks, 3 Ricks, 2 Vicks and someone called John!

Mick the Bomb was about 5' 9", clean shaven, and had an almost permanent smile on his face. He certainly was one for the women and was always chatting to some young woman he'd never met before, but in way like he had known them for years. He worked for Vettese's in the "middle" café on Regent Road as a Fryer, cooking up fish and chips for the hoards. It must have been about the same time that Vickie's brother, Albert Turner worked there, filleting and preparing fish. While sitting upstairs in the Big V one day, I saw some fool with a sheath knife he'd just bought from the shop along the road. Like a complete idiot he was threatening people and challenging any passers-by who looked at him. Albert went by. The fool challenged him "Come on mate, if you think you're hard enough!" Albert pointed at him, said wait there and ran across the road. The fool laughed, telling his audience how scared he makes people. 10 seconds later Albert reappeared with his fish filleting knife and said something like "We're even now son. You ready then?" The fool turned white, stammered, then ran off the other way, wisely!

Many people in those days used to carry knives, flick-knives or even old guns. Good grief, I can recall swapping guns and knives at school! Pocket Guns, little .22 revolvers, or even Derringer type guns, were easy to come by, you could buy them in junk shops even. Easy. So was ammo as you could collect dropped .22 rounds at the Fair! Though, different times back then. None of us had heard of "drugs" for a start. Were there any serious incidents? Not that I can recall.

It was in the Stagecoach Amusement Arcade one day that I met a bunch of lads on holiday. The four lads thought it would be good fun to go play football on the beach and say that they were a group called The Zombies. They said that I'd be their photographer pal, or some such ploy to pull girls. It never really worked but we did have fun. That was later, the summer of 1965 when The Zombies released "She's Not There" which rocketed up the charts.

That was such a warm summer, I spent much of it on the beach. In the picture above taken by me, you can see John "Frenchy" French sitting between a pair of sisters (sorry, can't remember names), one of whom was being a bit sassy, in the early summer of '64. No idea who the young man was on the right, I think he just joined us as he vaguely knew John or the girls (picture on previous page).

As they say "Tell you what though…" 1964 was a glorious summer. We used to have really cold winters and predictable summer heat waves then. Ideal for holidaymakers and locals alike to enjoy all that GY had to offer.

These Boots Weren't Made for Walking!
The Beatles' fashions continued. From Beatle Jackets to Beatle Suits and later, Beatle Boots (I think early 1964). These were in fact Cuban heeled boots. OK, high-heeled shoes! They were suddenly declared in fashion. Having never having seen anything like this before, and being a "short arse", I had to get some. Off I went to Martins Menswear in the Market Row and ordered a pair. A week later they were in. The salesman, who had seen me many times before by then, ushered me to the upstairs floor for boots and shoes. The price I cannot recall accurately,but around £14-£18 comes to mind; a lot of money then! "Here, take a seat

on the stool, opposite the mirror." He requested. Then got these huge black boots out of the box. The soles must have been 3" thick at least! He pulled the boots on for me, quite a struggle. Then said "Stand up, slowly." I stood up, slowly, but almost tipped forward head-first into the mirror, the heels were that high! Ha ha ha! He said (was it Chris?) "Don't worry, just keep your body up straight and you'll soon get used to them."

I wore those boots to the death, well, almost. But summertime came and I had to get some plimsolls. That was when I had that Achilles tendon problem and couldn't walk home.

Having been wearing the Cuban Heeled Beatle Boots all winter, I bought myself a pair of white plimsolls (a.k.a. "Tennis shoes"): we didn't have Trainers in those days! It was also a summer of romance too and there were many, many girls holidaying in Gt. Yarmouth who were looking for fun and summer flings. For almost two weeks that summer I spent with 'Mick the Bomb' and other mates, playing football on the beach or dating girls who were on holiday, or just knocking around with anyone you met and having a laugh.

The girls were quite bold then and would give you a warm smile, say hello and sometimes even beckon you over to them. They'd certainly let you know if they were interested in getting to know you: unlike women today who play silly games like pretending to be uninterested and then wondering why they are single! Most came down for holiday romances. Most of the two weeks was spent in caravans, but never the same one two nights running. If the girls were in a B&B, where guest were strictly not allowed, then I'd crash at Micky's place, just off Regent Road and we'd spend all day with them. If you wanted a bit of privacy you would ask them if they had seen "the dunes", which usually brought a smile, as they put there arm around your waist and said "Oh, that sounds exciting!" and off you went to the sand dunes at the northern end of Gt Yarmouth's beach.

Dosh.

Money was sometimes (usually) tight so when we were hungry we had "eggy dips" at Mick the Bomb's place, and if we were really lucky and had about 6d between us, a can of cold baked beans too! One hot and sunny day I was playing footy or Frisbee on the beach, near the Marina Centre. My Achilles Tendons suddenly both froze up in searing pain. This was because my tendons had "shrunk" while wearing the higher heeled boots, and now wearing flat shoes and doing lots of walking or playing, they went into spasm and seized. Literally I could not walk. Micky and another mate had to carry me to the Bus Stop, more or less by the Empire, and then, one each side, carried me home to 88 Lawn Avenue, the house I'd been born in. Somehow I got to bed and as soon as my head hit the pillow I was out to the world. When I awoke, it was just starting to get dark. My mother came up and brought me a cup of tea. "Oh, you're alive then?" I sat up, a bit tired and confused. Looking out of the window it seemed like I had been asleep for about 3-6 hours and had missed the rest of the day.

"Thanks I'm really thirsty. Have I been asleep all afternoon?" I asked her.

"*Afternoon*? Ha! You've been asleep for two-and-a-half-days boy!" came the shocking reply. I drank tea that she brought me, ate the meal she then cooked, and then slept some more that night before finally getting my act together and re-joining the summer throng. My mates were pleased to see me and we had a brilliant summer.

Being a seaside town, that's what summers were all about in Great Yarmouth. Cafes, beach, amusements arcades, music and of course holiday romances. We were also making up for extremely cold, dark, quiet winters when, most places were shut, and hardly a soul stirred or braved the cold easterly winds unless they really needed to.

(The picture above is one of my favourites and always makes me smile. This one dates to '65 and shows some of my old pals from those days: (Top) Tony Buck, Pat Weller, Clive Barron (?), John French (white Tee, leaning in) then Bryan Bream (centre) and Peter Scales (blacktop). Nobody seems to know who the young women are. Makes me smile though, you know, that smile you get when you remember good times with all your old mates.)

The rest of 1964 was a hazy, crazy mess of vague memories. Meetings by Juke Boxes in the Amusement Arcades, fun on the beach, riding here and there on my scooter. I met my mate Michael "Sandy" Sanderson (RIP) in 1964, we used to hang around together often and ride-off anywhere we fancied. Sandy was quite a one for the girls and had an ability to chat girls up, and I couldn't, so we often went out with local girls or holiday makers as they were usually in pairs. There were no serious relationships and usually not even kissing, just good friendships and having fun days out. Being free.

I think it was late '64 when I met Barry Green, who then introduced me to Tony & Ricky Elvin (older & younger brothers) who all lived in Newtown. We all became good mates and all lived close to each other. Gradually the "crowd" started to build and we all had so many mates that you could go somewhere with any of them on any day of the week. Often there was no "plan", you'd just go into town and meet-up randomly with whoever was there, and then do whatever ideas came along: usually going to another venue or sometimes a spontaneous trip out of town on our scooters. Tony, Ricky, Barry or "FIS" and me used to have quite a lot of adventures. One night I recall we'd "had a few" and one of them (I think Barry?) decided to get his scooter out, a Li "Slimstyle" and see if we could ride it with all four of us on it. The three of them managed to get on the seat and back carrier, while I sat on the front mudguard with my feet wrapped around the leg shields. We managed to get part way around the block, when the Barry decided to turn into an alley between the Newtown terraces. Over we went on the loose stones and the scooter skidded to a halt, my right ankle trapped underneath. Tony, Barry and Rick were in fits of hysteria after being thrown off the bike. Must admit, I was laughing too, after getting my leg out, but felt a bit painful. On pulling up my trouser cuff I looked, but at first couldn't see any problems. My red socks looked normal, but whoops, they were wet to the touch! In fact, there was a gaping hole on the outside of my sock as big as the circumference of a tea cup or mug! The accident had trapped my leg under the scooter and as it slid to a halt the stones had neatly taken out the side of my ankle, skin, blood vessels, the lot, and right down to the bone: which could be clearly seen by holding a cigarette lighter to it! That had me hobbling about for several weeks. Never bothered with hospitals or doctors. Wash it, bandage it and get on with life, there was a lot more to do! My family home had just moved to Caister-on-Sea then, due to Dad's ill health, and I recall hobbling back along Caister Road late at night, limping, in pain and the bleeding would start again as I walked the rough curb by the airfield. If anything, the pain and inconvenience just served to make me more resolute to get it healed and be able to get out and about "normally" again. After a month or so it started growing new skin over the bare bone. Amazing how over time though the body can cover a completely bare patch that size with new skin.

It wasn't until early 1965 that the Mod scene really started to kick off in Gt. Yarmouth. Stories had filtered through about the so-called 1964 "Bank Holiday Mod invasion" at Hastings, so many more young people wanted to be a part of this burgeoning group of fashionable young breakaways.

There was a bit of "aggro" in Great Yarmouth on Bank Holidays during 1964, so my new old pal, Richard Leavold, one of the old Anglo Rockers, told me. If you were in the wrong place at the wrong time, then you'd get caught up in it. Otherwise, blink and you'd miss it.

> Richard says "I remember it well, - 1964 is when it all kicked off in G.Y for us young'uns. I'd just started work, passed my motorcycle test on a B.S.A Bantam, sold it and bought my first Triumph, only

to have it kicked in by a gang of London Mods! I was devastated, but the bas-turds paid for it! Yes, 1964 through to 1967 are the years I remember well."

Gerry & the Pacemakers

Like I said elsewhere, it was only a very small minority who caused trouble, and usually from way outside of town as they thought they'd most likely be unrecognised by any locals. That is pretty much the same wherever you go, and especially in city nightclubs where gangs of young men with more testosterone than grey cells go deliberately to start a fight. I know this because one of my students became a 'Bouncer' and had to sort them out every week. He said they'd even punch female staff, so he was quite happy to go in and get them. He'd then come to the next training session and say "You know what we were doing in Taijiquan (or Kung-fu) last week? ... that works!"

How Do You Do It?

Music started to develop quickly too. *PACEMAKER*
Many new groups arrived on the scene
and what was different was new Record Labels were born.
These recording companies then scouted for new talent, like
The Beatles, Dave Clark Five and of course The Merseybeats,
who became popular almost overnight. Pictured below are
Gerry & The Pacemakers. In January 1965 (release date) they
starred in a film called "Ferry Across the Mersey" and in it rode
on old Lambrettas. That was a smash hit as they were already
one of the leading Mod bands and great Liverpool bands of the
time since 1963.

Consequentially, these lucky lads were all given a brand new
Lambretta (Series 3) which was, of course, a publicity stunt. The
scooter firm that did this quickly had some Transfers or badges
made up saying "Pacemaker" which was added to the 150 cc
Specials. The UK only Lambretta Pacemaker became a very
popular machine. In the film, 'Ferry Across the Mersey', Gerry
and the lads were seen riding older scooters off the ferry and to
someone's house, presumably for Band Practice. This was all
part of the popularity of scootering and Pop music. Scooters
were featured in many films during the 1960's, especially Italian
films as the humble scooter was just simply "a way of life" for
the masses, and far more popular than motorbikes.
The Cavern venue in Liverpool was made famous by these
bands. That was too far for us to go though, and why should we
when we had so much going on in Great Yarmouth! Telly wasn't
really a viable option in 1965. For a start it was black and white
(Mono), screens were usually about 8" to 10" diagonal, and
there were not many programmes on for young people. So
when 'Juke Box Jury' and 'Six-Five Special' came along, teenagers
were taking over mum and dad's TV set, much to their disgust at

this "modern music with words we can't understand"! Juke Box Jury was perhaps the most progressive of programmes as it featured a panel of teenagers who voted for new releases. There was one girl from Birmingham (Janice?) who started a catchphrase of "I'll give it five." Which sounded more like a nasally "Oil give it foive"! Later on the BBC decided to cash in with Top of the Pops. They featured live (or mimed) performances from groups or artists in the UK Top 20 hits charts. The only newspaper that teens were interested in was the NME or New Musical Express, not exactly a trendy name, but an informative read.

Woolworth's Label.

In Great Yarmouth, in those days, you had two choices if you wanted to buy the latest record. The best choice was to go to Arnolds Department Store (now Debenham's, if not closed!). There, in the cellar, was a dedicated corner for vinyl 45 RPM or 33 RPM records. They had two Preview Booths too where you could ask to hear part of the new record, go into the booth and put on the grubby earphones that hundreds of others had been wearing, then listen in private before deciding whether or not to buy it.

Option two was to go to Woolworth, by then in the Market Place. There, on the left-hand side of the store, not far from the door, was the Record counter. Woollies, as it was called by customers, used to hire copycat artists to make a record that sounded pretty much like the latest hits. These records were then sold cheaper than the real thing. Many young people, including myself, were happy to buy these, after all, it was the song we wanted more often than the original artist. Their record label was called 'Embassy' and they started that in the 1950's: a kind of precursor to Spotify, I guess. They always say there's nothing new in life, just borrowed from somewhere else. Their label was extremely popular, especially as it saved you money. Just look at this little reminder:

Priced at just 4/3d (21p in modern currency!) Come on boys and girls, dig them out from the loft, they'll be worth quids (£'s) by now!

You can check out the Woolworth Record storey by following this link: http://www.woolworthsmuseum.co.uk/1950s-embassyrecords.htm

They were the days when you'd go to your favourite place with a decent Juke Box to hear the latest hits in the Top Ten. Carefree days of teenage years.

Chapter 3:

1965: Rides and Rucks.

In 1965 we had the formation of the GY 65 CLUB – Great Yarmouth Scooter Boys. This was signalling the start of a boom, a big boom which saw many young men buy scooters. It was during the early spring that I was sitting on my Lambretta outside the Big V café and waiting…. and waiting, and waiting, for some other Mod on a scooter to come along and join me. I had just been to Norwich that week to buy my Parka. After a year of being a Mod and riding around during 1964 looking for other people on scooters, I had almost given up hope of ride-outs with other like-minded lads.

Eventually on a mild sunny Sunday, a lad came round the corner from the seafront and circled around beside me. I nodded and said hello.

He said "Hello mate. Are you a member of the GY 65 Club?" looking at the back of my Parka, which was blank. "No" I replied.
"You want to be?"
"Yeah, sounds good."
"OK," he said cheerily "Stick 'GY 65 CLUB' on the back of your Parka mate, 65 in a circle." (showing me the back of his Parka).

See you down here, or over the Chalet." And off he went. I went off to buy a big Marker Pen. A proper Club, wow!

My parents did question why I'd bough at huge Felt-tip pen and was writing on the back of my coat. They were probably thinking it was some gang or something. As it happened, I already knew of The Chalet Coffee Bar, in Gorleston. I had been going there for a year, on-and-off, but got fed-up with it as there were not many Mods going in there. Me, Sandy and a few others had been. But we were Yarmouth lads, so had plenty of hang-out choices anyway.

By the summer of 1965, you would see lots of Mods wearing a Parka. Parkas were ex-military clothing from the US Army. They were olive green, quite baggy, and had a hood and long tails which could potentially clip together under the crotch. The only place you could get your parka was at a local 'Army Surplus Store', a place of wonderment for those who had just missed compulsive call up or were not involved in war-like activities. Almost everything military can be found there with the exception of tanks and battleships. My mother used to hate my Parka. She shuddered at the thought of some American "Grunt" who had been wearing it and got shot at by Viet Kong, even though I cheerily explained "Look, it went through the tail-pieces, missed his body!" She was a very spiritual person though, and passed that on to me as I've had one after another experiences of the spirit kind!

It was in the Army Surplus shop on Dereham Road in Norwich (still there today) that I recollect browsing through many second-hand Parkas to try and find the best one for me and in my size, almost. The parkas generally had a few stitched up holes in them. These were from combat in Vietnam. Quite a few had holes in the front, about the chest area. One I saw had a neat group of three holes around the heart area. Poor sod, but at least he went quickly, some suffered long and agonising deaths. Mine had holes in the back, around and about arse level. This, I hoped, meant that the soldier had been sent home, injured but alive, or maybe he just had a lucky escape and near miss? We tried not to think too much about what injuries the original wearer befell at that time as it was not only uncomfortable but unimaginable. Only those who gone through the horrors of battle can know what it is really like, and then don't want to talk about it. Only the other day (2019) I was talking to a friend who had to shoot a SAS comrade in the head as he'd fallen into a Viet Kong trap, a pit with spikes in. He said it was either shoot him, as the injured soldier requested, or leave him to die slowly in agony, or if he survived, at the hands of the Viet Kong. No good choices. Mental scars last forever. Nowadays we call it PTSD, or Severe PTSD in some cases.

Before I got my Parka though, I'd bought a leather coat. It was a three-quarter length coat, black and double-breasted. It was Italian, of course. Having spent most of my formative years in short trousers, up until I was around thirteen or fourteen and very self-conscious, with girls staring up my loose trouser legs and commenting about the size of my balls hanging down my thigh it was really great to be able to wear some great fitting, well designed clothes and feel independent. That was one of the best things about Modernism, being able to express yourself by dressing up the way *you* wanted to. My leather coat went through many years with me and never went out of fashion. It was a classic.

My old leather coat saw some battles and misadventures too. It was handy having a leather coat on a scooter for those tiny little wheels seemed determined to throw you off the machine at almost any time, especially on sand drifted surfaces that we used to get in G.Y. all winter long. For example: One winter's day

I met a nice young lady who lived in one of the council houses down by the Fishwharfe. After meeting her in town, I arranged to pick her up on my scooter and take her to the cinema the following evening. In Gt. Yarmouth I had bought a pair of blood red coloured "Elephant Cord" jeans. Very trendy. My Italian leather coat and Parka atop, I set off that evening to collect her.

When I knocked at the front door I was confronted by a house full of women. Her mum, her sister/s, friends and lord knows who else were there, neighbours, the lot! They stood in the doorway, all staring at me: it was then I realized what animals at a zoo must feel like when a crowd suddenly gathers in front of their cage. She gave me a welcoming kiss then said "Oh, I'm not quite ready yet. Come in and wait." Knowing what was in store for me, and being a tad shy, I said "Tell you what, I'll go for a spin around the Harbour's Mouth and be back in about 10 minutes. Be ready, or we'll be late." Off I went. Past Birds Eye Foods, around the bend at the harbour and back along North Denes road towards the monument.

The lights on my scooter were very dim and only 6v. Suddenly the dim headlight beam lit up a patch of road that was yellowish. Sand drift! The front wheel literally skated off to the right and pitched the scooter over onto its left side in a second, throwing me over too. As it hit the road I saw a small lamp post ahead, the scooter looked doomed to head for it and crash. That I didn't want to happen, so as I rolled onto my left side, using the parka and leather coat to cushion my fall, I hooked my feet under the handlebars to slow the scooter down. A human anchor! It worked. I saved my poor old faithful LD from a far worse bashing. Trouble was, the concrete road had also ripped the side of my left knee out too. There was a gaping hole in the knee of my new jeans and matching coloured blood on my ripped skin. Nothing more to do, I checked the scooter for major damage, lo and behold, she was still alright to ride. What a relief. Brushed myself down, got on and went back to the girl's house. On opening the door, "they" were all still there and of course she noticed my injured leg. Her mum pushed forwards and looked at my leg. "Oh you poor thing" she said "Come in and I'll fix that leg up for you. Get those trousers off and I'll mend them too!" What? You cannot be serious?! Ha ha! Looking at the house full of concerned and excitable women I said "It's nothing. Come on, I'll be fine, let's go to the pictures!" And off we went.

They were very heady days indeed, 1965 and 1966 especially. There were times when I was very, very glad that I had both my Italian leather coat and my Parka. We didn't have any proper clothing for motorcycle or scooter riders in those days, so you just wore whatever you had. There were very few helmets about, but we didn't want to wear them anyway. As for gloves... you either wore leather gloves, which got wet and froze solid in winter, or woollen gloves, which were not much better. Woollen gloves were better for clutch lever work as leather gloves tended to have four stitching ridges in each finger that were awkward to grip in, to say the least. Nothing stopped me riding my scooter, snow, fog (couldn't see a damned thing!) or hale, oh the joy!

The Famous Five Ride Out!
Never mind the Famous Five, the famous '65 Boys' were the ones to watch! One dull evening, either in Spring or Autumn, five of us, each on his own machine, headed towards the Wellington Pier and beyond to the South Denes Caravan site. There was nothing doing, nobody around and not even a solitary car on the road. We who smoked had just lit up a roll-up, but decided we'd head back towards Regent Road. It seemed easier to smoke and chat on the way back, so I thought, if we sat back

on the pillion seat (we all had rear carriers with back-rests on) and put the feet over the handlebars to control steering and keep the throttle open, we could cruise back and chat with ease. The other lads thought this was a great idea, so off we set, got up to about 20 in 2nd or 3rd gear (depending on gearing) and headed back, sitting back, feet up and having a chat as we rode. Can you imagine what would happen if you did that nowadays?

Timber!
That wasn't the only trick we got up to either. Jewsons Timber yards on Southtown Road, had gates all the way down. Timber was stacked in rows going from the road end to the river end, so the gates gave them access to each aisle of timber stacks. They had some large Timber Grab Trucks which would drive over a pile of timber, lower the grabs, then hoist it up underneath. They would then drive out of the yard via one gate and along Southtown Road, turning into another gate. This could be quite hazardous for traffic. The empty wagons would then go back out along the road to pick up another load. That's when another great idea struck me.

There were again about five scooters. All heading towards The Chalet from GY. As I saw the empty truck turnout onto Southtown Road, I noted that it was about the right height to ride under, if you kept your head down. The next gate was still a way off, so I opened up and went for it, whizzing through underneath the big machine. As I popped out in front and looked back over my shoulder, I saw some of the other lads lining up for it and the driver, waving his fist at me. A couple of other got through before he turned into the next gate. Daredevil teenage years, eh?

Overall we were safe and good drivers, we had to be. Scooters are not as easy to ride as motorbikes, the latter suffering more from speed issues rather than stability issues with smaller wheels or poor brakes. We also wore no crash helmets, or "skid lids" as we called them. I'll swear my head has saved me several times in falls and spills!

Of course, if you had a lovely young "Modette" on the back, then you would be even more careful. As you can see by this picture, if you were to crash her legs would most certainly bear the brunt of the fall and be ripped by the road surfaces. We had respect for our women counterparts in those days. Remember though, we had some really nice clothes on too, so the last thing we wanted to do was crash and end up looking like a bloody scarecrow!

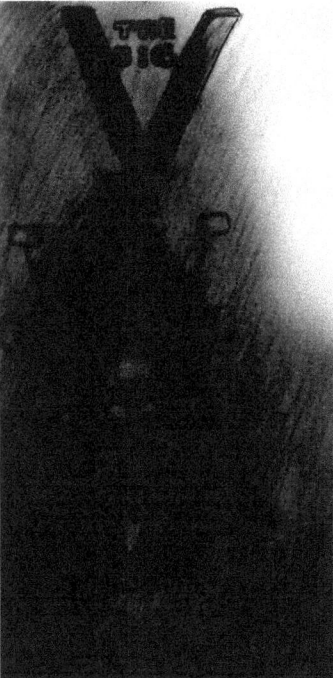

The Mod girls were a funny lot. Some used to drift from one lad to another, mostly, just being with whoever they thought was trendy that week or whoever they thought had a nice scooter. Life was fairly simple like that and I think most of us saw them as friends, or part of the group, not just "birds", but there's always the odd few males or females who see, conquer and move on to the next notch in the bedpost. Never my style and I probably ignored more "opportunities" than many lads would have loved to have had.

Henry 'Lord Harry' Manguzi draws this marvellous picture for us in 2019 and recalls:

"A cup of coffee at the big V put a couple of songs on the juke box's on a cold winters night with your mates, pop up to the bowling alley park our scooters outside on the road chat for a while then go in the alley to get warm . Then pop in for a burger at the wimpy Bar , and. Then a ride over with half a Dozen mates on their scooters to The Chalet at Gorleston. My first scooter an Old Vespa 125 cost me £15 second hand and very old . When I went out on it I thought I was the dogs bollocks. how times have changed!"

You are so very right there mate. Not one of us knew what the future would hold or even if we had a future, but here we are. In fact I doubt that any of us even thought about the future, being so busy living life to the full!

Thanks for the drawing 'Harry'. You are now "immortal"!
(*Sent in earlier, just two months before we had the sad news.*)

"Harry" was one of the Five. Not a rowdy fella, nor loud. He was quiet, but also great fun, always cheerful and smiling. We had some harmless but fun times on our scooters as well as in the coffee bars. Great chats and even greater ride-outs.

Another picture (below) to bring a smile to your face. Nine of the lads one night outside of The Chalet Coffee Bar in Gorleston. I can only name three or four of them, see if you can get them all.

Names L-to-R: _____

_____

_____

Icy Trips.

Again, I can't remember why, but I had been to Norwich on a cold winter's day. As I returned it was snowing, with a little sleet for that extra face punishment from the Easterly wind driving it into me. I had donned my woollen gloves, scarf around the mouth, Parka done up as much as possible, pulled the hood up, and tied the tails under my backside and rode a long, slow journey home. It was a long journey, bitterly cold and hardly any other traffic was on the roads. The Acle Straight was almost deserted, save for a couple of cars going the other way, one that passed me, and me, a mad Mod on a 150 scooter!

As I approached Gt. Yarmouth along the last mile or so of The Acle Straight, I noted the deepening pile of snow in my lap, the ice that had woven itself into my woollen gloves and the fact that I could barely feel my hands at all, they were frozen stiff, numb and senseless. Then the thought struck me, "How the hell am I going to change gears and slow down as I approach the bridge?" Somehow, and with a lot of willpower, I managed to wiggle my fingers free from the clutch and eventually move my fingers. The LDb only had three gears, so changing down to second was all that was needed for a careful and steady transition of the old Vauxhall Bridge. The roads were pretty barren of other transport, so I guess I was the only one mad enough to be out on two wheels in that weather! From Vauxhall Bridge it was straight along Lawn Avenue, then attempting a frozen dismount when home. It must have taken me ages to thaw out when I got home though.

My mother thought I was totally mad. My father thought it was quite normal, as it's what he would have done. He never said anything, but knowing my Dad, he probably thought "That's my boy!"

Young Friends.

That period of time, 1963 to 1966, was quite amazing insomuch as virtually anyone would talk to anyone else. Great Yarmouth was packed in the summer and it seemed like everyone was out and about. If you met someone you talked to them. Simple as that. My mates at the time included Joe Cuttajar (63-64), Tony and Ricky Elvin, Barry Green, Bernie Shepherd, Dave Williams (RIP), Teddy Griffin, John 'Frenchy' French, Michael "Sandy" Sanderson (RIP), Henry "Lord Harry" Manguzi (RIP), Andy Perdicou (RIP), Barry Pigano, Greg Long, occasionally Vicky Turner, 'Muggy' Driver (RIP) - around '64 to '65, then mainly, around '66 I think Tony Buck, John Cemelli, some of "The Cross Boys",, Brian Harden, Pete 'Peewee' Rouse (later), and again scooter boys Arthur Skippen, Micky Devlin, Bryan Bream, Alan Virgin, Steve Hornigold, Chris Pretty, Pete Allard, Brian "Churchie" Church, John Nockolds, John Driver and many, many more: we'd gather randomly and go for spontaneous ride-outs together.

It has been estimated, at one meeting in The Chalet, that there was around 220 'GY 65 CLUB' members between 1965 and 1967. That's one heck of a club. There were no numbered cards, fees, badges or stickers, just the ubiquitous "GY 65 CLUB" written on the backs of our Parkas and the occasion "65" stickers on a scooter side-panel. The best part of it though is that many of us are still going strong and meeting up on a regular basis and still at the same place too.

We've had some great reunions so far. Next one, as this book is written, should be on Friday 9thAugust 2019, around 10 am to 1pm at The Chalet Coffee Bar, Lowestoft Road, Gorleston-on-Sea, Norfolk. If readers know of any expatriated Gt Yarmouth Mods of the 60's, please do let them know. It's open to all though, whether "65 Boys", girls, Mods, Rockers, anyone who visited Great Yarmouth in those days.

Barry Green > Chuchie > Sandy > Ricky > Arthur.
GY Scooter Boys in Taunton c.1966.

In both 1965 and 1966 my summers were rudely disturbed by that four letter word "work", so I missed loads of scooter trips with my pals, like the one to the south-west country with Churchie, Barry, Arthur, Sandy, Tony and Ricky (See picture above). These fellas were some of my best mates in those days, so I was somewhat disappointed that I couldn't make the trip. Neither Lacon's Brewery nor Bird's Eye Foods took too kindly to absenteeism! (I worked at both places during this period after leaving Grouts at 18 because I didn't want to do the Three Shifts routine – they found me a job working days for a while, but I got tired of an idiot I worked with, Ernie, who used to wind me up all the time. I did get a rollicking for it once when I offered him out on the roof to settle it and he chickened out, but then reported me! (What a low-life creep.) I think that was early '65 and I eventually left to work at Birds Eye Foods factory, much better pay, but shifts again.

My old school mate, Dave Williams, was "one of the lads" then. He was a big lad for his age. In fact, when he was at school, in my class, still just 15, he was being taken out to Night Clubs by two 21 year old glamorous woman in a sports car. Then they used to take him back to their place, apparently, and sometimes drop him off at school in the morning. I guess that makes those women paedophiles by today's standards! From what I saw, there were quite *a lot* of older women seeing teenage lads in those days. We never hear of them getting into trouble with the law do we? Only the men who get seduced by younger girls: and even then the younger girls don't get into trouble either. How biased and sexist British *'law and disorder'* is!

What a great bunch of blokes my mates were though, then and now. I'm sure that not one of the lads would have anything bad to say about any of the "GY 65 Boys". We all got on pretty well and used to mix well too. Call me slow, but it was only recently that I discovered one of Dave's relatives on Facebook. She had mentioned Dave. In chat, I discovered that Dave's father was non-other than Vince Williams, a local Judo and Aikido Sensei (Teacher). Around 1973 I had been invited to train privately with three Budoka (students of Japanese Martial Arts, or Bu Do), Kevin Addy, "Tramp" and "Trim". Kevin became my "Martial Brother" and we had some great times training together. He told his teacher, Sensei Vince Williams about me and I was then invited to go see him at his home in Gorleston. What a terrific man he was and we got on just great. Never once did I connect Dave Williams with him though, even though Dave could handle himself if he needed to. As an aside, I saw Sensei Williams in a Demo at the Floral Hall one time. He performed some Aikido techniques and, for a man who normally walked like a coalman, he moved very swiftly and gracefully indeed.

Staircase.

By the mid-sixties though many of us were playing in our own

groups. Some followed Pop (Popular Music: the Top 20, etc.) while others went Rock or Blues. It was during the latter part of 1966 and early '67 that I sang in a band called 'Staircase'. The dates I may have a bit muddled. My hazy memory of those hectic and dizzy times does not allow me to recall the precise line-ups at precise times. However, we do have just one picture of the group, taken c.1966 at the Sandringham Hotel, owned by Ted Lees. The Sandringham was a very large hotel, just opposite the Aquarium Cinema. We played in the cellar room, which was large dining area, with bar, dance floor and stage. Hotel guests would stay at Great Yarmouth all week, then on a Friday night we would play all kinds of Pop, Rock and Blues to give them a good farewell evening. Ted Lees had two sons, who we knew, and they did suggest that we were kept on for such a long time because we offered the best variety of music for a good night's entertainment and we were consistently good. Fair compliments

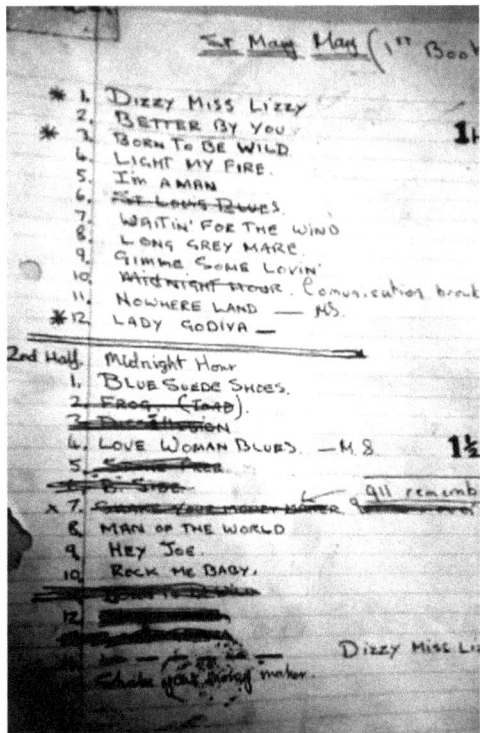

indeed, seeing as how many groups there were around that time! The line-up above: Left, Dave "Twisty" Askew on Keyboard, Peter "Peewee" Rouse on Bass Guitar, Paul Goodwin on Percussion, Michael "Paddy" Trannah as Backing Vocalist (at that time), Myke "Lucky" Symonds as Lead Vocalist on the far right. This photo was taken, we think, at a girl's 21st birthday party (Janice Humberstone), by her. We are really grateful to her for taking some photo's as none of us ever did. That was the thing about that time, we just did what we enjoyed.

Here is my only remaining trace of Staircase, a song list: I used to do these at home as either the rest of the band were too busy or couldn't be bothered, but if I did it we had a fair choice from all band members of the numbers they liked. Keeps the peace and provides variety.

It says "1st Booking" on the top right, but I suspect it may have been a first at that particular venue... wherever that was (not same as the party, above.) Mick "Paddy" Trannah came in as backing vocals for a while. Like I said, there were many comings and goings. For amusement I jammed at parties, mainly around Caister-on-Sea way as we had to move there when my Dad became really ill. There was a guitarist named Mick, from

Caister-on-Sea I used to jam with and even wrote him and his mates a couple of songs. As "payment" he made me a huge brass belt-buckle with brass Bolt-heads in it, on a woven leather belt. I wore that for years! The belt eventually rotted, but I still have the buckle... somewhere.

Among the listings were just two of my own songs, "Love Woman Blues" plus "Nowhere Land" and Fleetwood Mac's "Man of the World", Hendrix's "Hey Jo" and "Shake your money maker" so you can see we were leaning towards a slightly different direction than most bands. We liked many Album Tracks, as did members of the general public too of course. That trend carried forward later into Snake Disco, down in the cellar bar at the Royal Hotel. They were fun nights too.

Ironically, this past Xmas day (2018) I dug out some of my old lyrics and put together a cheap Home Studio set-up. I recorded one on the 25th December 2019 called "Shadows (of the past)". The original was only two scribbled verses, but I changed that on-the-fly and added some more, making it a sad and sentimental love song. The next one might be "Nowhere Land", we shall see.

Ted Lees, who owned the Sandringham Hotel, gave us one of the best tips a band could have: "Always slowdown in the middle, so they can dance. Then for the last number, leave them rocking so they'll want more"! It worked. That summer season was hard work, especially as most of us worked all day too. Having less photos of the sixties than Punk Records on Desert island Discs (you'll need to be an old fart to remember that one!) I was surprised to find not only a picture of the poster for the Tower Ballroom (with our band on it) but an old song list from those heady days. It was left pretty much up to me to make or change the list, the Set, but I used to ask the others what they wanted in it and we would get 3 or so songs/numbers that would suit us individually while pleasing the general public too.

Tower Ballroom.

One of the last gigs I did was at the Tower, a charity gig organised by a 14 year old Kate Newlyn of Burgh Road, Gorleston (see newspaper clipping). Almost a claim to fame! Staircase had developed a few "wobbles" at that time and a few loose treads, so I formed a new band called 'Berlin' especially for the event. That went down a storm, or should I say "Blitzkrieg"?!

It was some time not long after that gig that I was invited to do another one up there (Tower) with another well known local band, Generous Earth. The lead guitarist was Roy Bruda, an amazing player. I can recall when he first started playing. I went over to his house in Gorleston, well, almost Bradwell, not far from the high School. He said "Hey, look at this Lucky." and showed me an electric guitar, a Fender Stratocaster, or "Strat" as they became known. He told me that it had been damaged and how he just wanted to rebuild it. He had neither musical instrument knowledge or musical training. He picked up the guitar and just played it by ear, copying Hendrix and other great guitarist's riffs. I was amazed by that. Anyway, that charity gig was a bit later, possibly late '66 or early '67 before I went to Leicester. The drummer was Clifford "Monty" Montague (RIP) and,

KATE SHOWS THE WAY

Entirely on her own initiative, 14-year-old Kate Newlyn, of 97, Burgh Road, Gorleston, organised an ambitious charity dance at the Tower Ballroom on Friday and raised £120 5s. for Shelter.

This was Kate's second dance in aid of Shelter. The first, a few weeks ago, raised £32. Encouraged by her success Kate decided to organise a bigger money-spinning project.

Her three weeks of intensive effort—booking six local groups and negotiating for the hire of the ballroom—paid off and resulted in a highly successful dance which was attended by over 650 young people.

The six pop groups—Staircase and Berlin (Yarmouth), Design for Living (Blundeston), Storm (Lowestoft), Kochbacher (south-wold) and Splinters (Gorleston) all played free of charge.

The ballroom was let at a specially reduced rate so Kate could raise as much money as possible from the dance for Shelter.

I'm thinking that at that time the Bass player was named Hughes, but we called him "Hugsy". One number we did that night was a "shocking" take on Blue Suede Shoes, one of my pee-takes on society and the drug scene at that time: a lot of people were taking prescription drugs called "blues".

Lyrics went something like this:
"Well...
You can knock me down,
Step on my face,
Slander my name all over the place.
You can do these things, 'cos your the Fuzz
But lay off a my dubes 'cos I need a buzz.
Who-oh yeah, and a pick-me-up!"

Went down well with the younger audience, but not so welcomed by the Drug Squad who were in the crowded ballroom. No ruddy sense of humour some people!

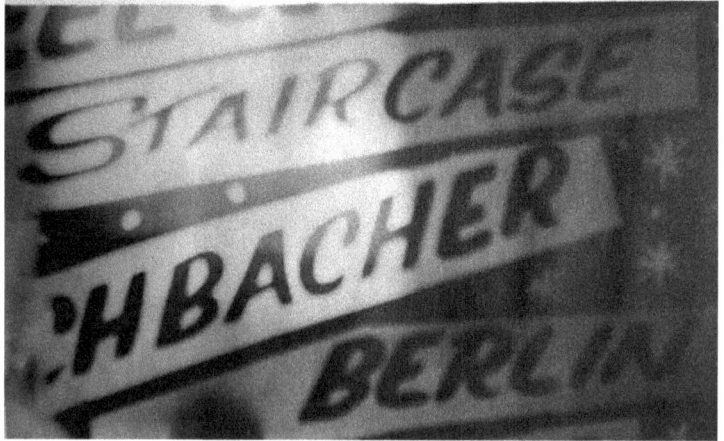

Rock 'n' Rolling on.

The band 'Staircase' was still rocking and rolling on. At one time we had Dave "Porky" Pigford (RIP) on Rhythm Guitar and we had a *string* of lead guitarists (see what I did there?), as Lead Guitarists were generally a funny old lot and found it hard to settle in one place. Kev "Milord" Claxton (now in Jaques de Ladd) came in with us later on, and that brought in some different material, as all musicians have their preferences in musical taste. The summer season at the Sandringham Hotel continued to be our "bread and butter". Then we took on such giddy heights as Caister Youth Club, the Green Gate pub and various party events. We did make it to the Tower Ballroom though, where in the mid 60's the Who played, alongside many other big name local or regional bands. Many of the local bands did a charity gig there and they were well attended and very popular. Sometime later (67/68?) I formed a band called 'Berlin' just for one such charity event there and sang a song I wrote of the same title: basically giving the view that thousands of innocent people also died when Berlin was bombed and that war was two-sides of a coin, not one. Innocent people die in any war torn country. On the same bill were a re-formed Staircase and Kochbacher (it was common for groups to split up and reform under another name, mixing members at the same time. There were so many musicians in Great Yarmouth at that time that bands used to form and split again within weeks, let alone months, so Staircase lasting two years was pretty good. Sadly Staircase didn't last very long after that night, nor did Berlin. In fact I lost interest in singing in 1967/8 as there were too many clashes of characters around.

Another one of my connections was with a couple of the members of the local band called "Excalibur": Tony Walsh, David Mason, Jim Hewkin and Tom Hewkin. They decided that the big time for them would come if they sank all their money into making a L.P. Record. So they did, at Scratby Recording Studios. I can still visualize the place, in a loft of a Chalet-style house. In fact, I bought one of their LP's, "Excalibur Rising", one of just 99 made – they settled for 99 as the price went too high for over

100! The album was so basic that the Jacket was not even glued together, to make a "slot", like normally happens. But it was well pressed vinyl and I still have it, unscathed, sounds perfectly clear too (played twice!).

If you want the URL for tracing 'Music from the East Zone', here it is: http://www.musicfromtheeastzone.co.uk/bands_artists/EXCALI BUR.htm

Oh bla di, oh bla dah, life goes on… yeah!
The weeks of '66 were mostly taken up with work and at Bird's Eye Foods at that time. When I first started at Bird's Eye it was to take my driving test, not in a car, but on Fork Trucks. These things are heavy and lethal if they hit you, so you have to be able to handle them to the required standards. Having passed my Scooter Test first time, then Fork Truck, they then wanted me to take the Brush Truck Test too. These were far more difficult to drive as the driver sits in a little bull-nose cockpit at the front and the much wider forks are behind you, protected by a thick outer wing to protect the loads. As you can imagine, getting through doorways and along aisles was a skill in itself. Having passed that test first time they let me loose on the factory floors and yards, shifting loads from one place to another. Later though I got placed in The Swedish Tunnel. Sounds grand, eh? All they did there was to "rehydrate" peas: a clever name for adding a second layer of frozen water, which of course made them heavier.

Working at Bird's Eye was one of the things that both helped me and hindered me. During the time I was with Staircase, we *needed* to have band practice at least 2-3 times weekly. In 1965-66 I was working 12 hour days though, plus Saturday morning too. As I was, in theory, nearest to the place we used to store our gear and rehearse in, it was my chore on a Friday evening to finish work at 6 pm, take the ferry across the merse... oh, sorry, across the Yare, then walk all the way from Ferryside to a junior school near The Chalet Coffee Bar, where our gear was. The Caretaker would let me in to the small side-hall (on the right), where I would then set-up the Amps ready for when the rest of the lads got there about 6:45 to 7 pm. We'd then practice until about 10 pm, pack up and head off home. In my case home was Caister-on-Sea, so Twisty used to give me a lift. We became fairly good mates that way. Little did I realise then that my first born daughter would go to that same school some 20 years later.

Sometimes I'd see Twisty for a pint on odd evenings when we had nothing to do. It was one such evening that we met Becky and her mate from Leeds, who were on holiday. She was a lovely young woman. I wonder what became of her. Twisty had a old Ford Anglia van at that time. That was a horror, especially when it was raining. There was something, shorting in the electrical department. If he turned on the radio the windscreen wipers started, if he turned on the heater, something else went!

We saw Becky and her mate at the Palmers Bus Stop. They stared, smiled and waved as we went past. I told him to go past again. We did, and stopped. We gave them a lift to Newtown, where they were staying. After making a date to see them again, we set-off to spruce up. After a good first night out we started talking to the girls about UFO sightings - don't ask how that came up! So after the Pub we parked up in a dark lane somewhere along Winterton cliffs, or that way. I was in the back with Becky. We stared and stared at the night sky as we chatted too. In the dark we could just make out a very vague cliff edge and sea. Ahead was a gate and hedgerow. After a while a bright light appeared in the night sky, coming from the west. It was further back, but looked almost parallel to the hedgerow, but 60-90 feet above. We all gasped "Look. There's one!" as it stopped and hovered silently. Although we said it was a UFO I thought it was one of their new helicopters from Caister Airfield, recently converted for servicing the Oil Trade in G.Y. The girls were excited. We watched as it stayed still, the bright spotlight looking down on the cliffs somewhere south of our position (image below left). Just as I was certain that it was a helicopter, but not saying anything to disappoint the others, the light suddenly, and I mean *very* quickly, shot up and backwards at a 45° angle, accelerating to what looked like 800 to 1000 mph plus and vanishing beyond the clouds in a second! (Image reproduced below right) UFO it was then! There have not been as many UFO sightings in Norfolk as elsewhere, but that was the second one I had seen up until then. The first was in 1963, above the town; also spotted by an ex-RAF man who reported it.

Later on, 1966 methinks, I was doing three shifts at Bird's Eye Foods and that was hard work. Somehow though I still managed to pack in a social life and a girlfriend too! At that time I met Julie who was a steady girlfriend for quite some time to come. Though we did split up for a while in '67, which made me decide to clear off to Leicester with my mates Tony & Ricky Elvin: we'd both had arguments with parents, so got packed that night, and off we went in 1967 top Leicester (see story above). Tony was the older brother and very serious, whereas Ricky a couple of years younger but liked to have fun. Often we'd all go out to the pub together, sometimes with Barry Green too.

Summer Love.
It was with Tony & Ricky one night, at the pub opposite the Jetty, we had a quiet night out in the summer. It was a Friday night. As we left, three girls were walking along the opposite side of the road and noticed us leaving the pub. They shouted and waved, so we crossed over and met-up with them. They were staying at a caravan in Caister-on-Sea, with another girl (she was out with a bloke who had a motorbike). We walked them home. They had not had a very lucky week when it came to holiday romances though and (in retrospect) wanted to make up for it. We stayed. Miss 'R', who took a shine to me, and me to her, was a very pleasant young woman with rosy cheeks, dark wavy hair and a gorgeous smile. Their mate rambled back not long after us, very drunk. She had to be put to bed as she was totally wasted. I recall that she looked very much like a young Bridgette Bardot and even wore a pink gingham dress. Very nice. It was an awkward arrangement that night, but we managed to split a double bed into two, with us on one side, Tony and his young woman on the other, separated only be sheets. Miss R managed to keep me at it all night long, and I mean *all night*! Ricky and his girl had the single bed on the other side of the van. The next morning we said our goodbyes and 'R' said that she'd wished we had met up earlier. They got a taxi to the station and headed back to Manchester way. Me, Tony and Ricky walked back home and caught up on some well-deserved sleep! We never heard from them again as we'd completely forgotten to ask for addresses in the heat of the moment and rushed goodbyes. We were pretty tired too, after being up all night. That was the summer of 1965, a summer of fun on the

beach, amusement arcades and drinking out with our mates. There were many more encounters and escapades.

Fair Do's.

That's just reminded me of another brief encounter around that time. Me and another of the "65 boys" were sitting outside the Regent Bowl on our scooters, feet up on the hgandlebars, as you do. It was a dull early spring evening and barely a mouse stirred. The Travelling Fair had just started arriving in GY for what we called "the Easter Fair", and were setting up their rides and stalls. A tall young woman walked down Regent Road, on the opposite side to us. There was nobody else about. She was looking at me as she got closer. I was looking at here too. She was around 6' 1" tall, wearing a biker's Leather Jacket and jeans. She had long dark wavy hair and was quite attractive. We just stared at each other. As she got closer she started crossing the road, making a bee-line for me. She spoke first, saying "You're not so bad looking for a Mod!" I smiled, "And you're not so bad looking either, for a Rocker." I joked.
She stopped in front of me, still with the unbroken stare. She gave a little smile. "Alright then. How'd you fancy a walk down to the beach with me then?"
I looked her up and down and said "Yeah, OK. Let me put my scooter away first though." She waited while I wheeled my LDb down the alleyway and parked it on the back road: something we'd do to be cautious when there were not too many people about or when the town attracted many visitors, among them thieves! We didn't say much. She told me that she was with the Fair, didn't have a boyfriend and had not had sex for a couple of months, but saw me and wanted to have sex with me. She seemed like a straight-forward and honest young woman. I like girls like that: straight-forward, honest and uncomplicated! We walked and swapped some idle chat and she led me under the Britania Pier. I'd better end the story there! That sort of thing,

"things that go bump in the night", happens very rarely in life.

By the time I got back there was nothing at all going on. Nobody at "the bowl" (Bowling Alley) so I got my trusty scooter and headed for home. GY has always been a town of contrasts, ultra-busy in summer, dead as door nails in winter. It used to start building up at Easter and last until the end of August, the main season. In winter there were very few places open, so it was quite boring for us teens.

The Trips I missed.
Not only did I miss out on the Cornwall trip due to work, but 2-3 other memorable trips too, again due to work and weekend shift overlaps or over-time. The Crystal Palace trip was one. These seem to be the only ones my mates took photographs of too. Days off were still fun though. When those lads were not about there were plenty of other characters to hang-out with.

The 'GY 65 CLUB' Crystal Palace Trip:
On the trip: (as sent in by one of the lads, Peter Allard) "from right to left, I hope, is Alan Virgin, Nick Ash, Chris Patterson, Bryan Bream, Graham Jackson, John Driver, Mick Reid, John Cook, Tony Buck, not sure who the one above is, then Richard Stuart, Mac Powsey, don't know the next two then Bryan Bream, the last one

I can't make out." Others were on that trip, such as Chris Baker-Pretty and whoever was taking the photo. Although it may be hard to make out faces and put names to them, it is so good to see that these pictures have emerged.

Part of the reason for writing this "memory lane" book was to preserve as much history as possible for our children, their children and future generations.

It was a big shame that I missed those trips, but unlike some, I had to work on Saturdays. There were many other adventures though and I did have fun. My trips to Leicester were between jobs though, so were varied in length of time I stayed.

Still, I did have many "Ride-outs" with the lads, or varied groups of them, when I didn't have to work weekends. They were all enjoyable times.

The most pleasant memories for me was when a group of us decided to ride-out somewhere, me hanging back a bit in the middle and just absorbing the sights and sounds of all those beautiful scooters with their colours, chrome and different exhaust sounds. Yes, I even liked the smell of Two-Stroke!

Trips and Troubles.

There were many an occasion when, on a Saturday, we would meet up outside of either the Ten Pin Bowling Alley, our "secret car park" or outside Woolworth's in Gt. Yarmouth market place. It wasn't a regular spot, just one of the places where we could "possibly" meet up. Basically, if you saw another scooter with Mod on-board you'd just stop, park up and chat. Sooner or later there would be others coming along and joining the group. It was on one such occasion, on a sunny Saturday, outside "Woollies" the group became about twenty scooters. What a sight to behold! Chrome, beautiful paintwork, mirrors and lights, racks and aerials with either pennants or tails on. Many a Lambretta and Vespa scooters. Someone would then shout "I'm bored" then a consensual murmur and "Let's ride somewhere" Short pause. "Let's go to Clacton!" and off we all went. As we all started off, I used to hold back just a bit, right in the middle of the pack, so that all the scooters would pass me on either side as we set off. I can still visualise it, the sight, the sound, the smell of Two-Stroke exhaust. Ah, sheer bliss! Off we went to Clacton, or wherever, with no thought about the how's why's or wherefores' we just enjoyed the ride. One such day in Clacton I met a petite blonde girl, "M". She was a Mod. We got on alright so I arranged to see her the next weekend. The picture on the left is one of her taken, I think, in a Photo-Booth, another popular invention of the 60's that we used to use a lot, just for fun and just because we could.

That weekend, having no overtime to do, I set off, packing a sleeping bag on the rear carrier with a change of socks and pants, Tee-shirt, etcetera. I left on the Friday evening, so I could spend all day Saturday with her. As it got dark, somewhere on route, on the A12, I parked up behind a hedgerow on the grassy end of a field. Got my sleeping bag out, climbed in, zipped up and covered my face with the hood, and nodded off. Next morning I awoke and thought it was starting to rain. "Pat... pat..... Pitter-patter" sound of what I thought were drops of rain. On carefully removing the hood, I saw a fat little field mouse jumping off my bag and scurrying away, stopping briefly for a moment to turn and look over his shoulder at me. I imagined that if he could speak he was thinking "Wow! That's weird. That mound moves and has a face!" After packing away I continued my journey to Clacton.

Miss 'M' was pleased to see me and we spent a good day together. I did pull her up on one issue though as she took the pee out of someone with a mental handicap. That's not on, then, now or ever. After that she settled down and became more thoughtful. On Saturday nights I slept in a seafront shelter, seaward side, out of the wind. I say "slept", eventually out of exhaustion as the seat was so uncomfortable it hurt. It was one of those "S" shaped wooden slat seats. In the morning I'd awake with all sorts of aches and pains. Stretch, then look for somewhere to get a cuppa and something to eat. Clacton, despite all the newspaper lies, was a fairly quiet place with a large percentage of older people. Occasionally I saw the odd Mod here and there, the odd Rocker too, but nobody ever gave me any hassle. In fact I'd leave my scooter all day or all night on the seafront and it never got touched by anyone. Several weekends were spent in Clacton, with her. I recall that as we got closer, several weekends in, and more "romantic" you might say, we were walking towards the beach one day where there was a Board Walk. She had her arm around my waste and her left hand in my back pocket, we kissed... again, and I said "Your jeans are coming down" She looked and said "They're not." My reply was "Oh yes they are, I've made my mind up!" Oh such wit! Off we went to make love under the boardwalk. Hence when I hear that song, "Under the Boardwalk" I always smile and think of my friend from Clacton.

There was one weekend trip to Clacton when I ran out of petrol and money, so could not get home. I had to walk several miles to find a Police House, on the A12 I think, and ask the man to telephone my father, who then gave him details and eventually got a loan of 30/- (30 shillings, or One Pound & Ten Shillings or £1.50 pence now) to get a cuppa, a roll and petrol for the trip home. Then of course I had to walk back to the scooter, finally pushing it to the nearest petrol station: which wasn't "near" at all. That was on a Sunday, and I had to walk quite some way to achieve that goal! That taught me a lesson: check pockets! If I remember rightly, about a month later, Miss 'M' met someone more local, so we put it down to experience and agreed not to see each other again and that was my last trip to Clacton. It wasn't a very exciting place to be anyway, mainly retired folk and not much for younger people to do. Apart from the romantic interlude, my main memory of Clacton was the main road down to the seafront. That was a nightmare to drive along and had many side roads cutting across at angles. Many car drivers would cut across in front of you without even looking, or just not caring.

The Crash.
It was on a day when I was working (again!) that a large group of the lads decided that they would go to Clacton. Among the group were the "faster lads" on their Lambretta GT200's with rapid acceleration and "modern" disc brakes. Among these were 'Ginger'*, with Sonia as pillion rider (*Ginger was not an insult,

like considered nowadays, it was just a statement of fact and an affectionate nickname, like "Blondie", nothing negative was meant by it). They both wore crash helmets, which was unusual in those days. The journey then was on the old road and that took them through the village of Yoxford. Just at the centre of the village was a notorious bend, it was a hairpin bend: A straight approach with a "U-shaped" bend by the village sign on a triangular patch of grass. Ginger and the other GT riders were racing. Ginger sped into the bend and lost control. Keith's scooter mounted the grass island and the front wheel hit a concrete filled, steel tubular signpost straight on. This catapulted both over the handlebars and into the post, both their heads smacking into the post at about 50-60 mph. Both crash helmets split wide open! Sonia had hair-grips in her hair and these were pushed through her scalp and into her brain. She had to have a very serious operation and ended up having a metal plate placed in her skull to protect her brain afterwards. Ginger was thought to be dead at first. He was severely comatose. He remained that way in hospital for several months, I think about three. Recently I have heard that he survived, thankfully, and later migrated to Australia. Sonia, bless her, a lovely and lively young woman, used to act a bit "strange" sometimes and we figured that it must have been because of the damage she sustained. We were all deeply shocked by the news. I think that it even slowed down some of the boys on their GT's, to a degree or two. Even Greg.

Sitting On the Dock of the Bay.
One Sunday in that year, a mate and I decided we wanted to ride down to Felixstowe, just for the sake of it. He was on Pillion. We got as far as Felixstowe Docks in the afternoon when we saw a Ferry. It said on the sign "Regular Return Trips to Harwich". As neither of us had been to Harwich we thought that it would be a great idea. So we boarded the ferry and were off, leaving the scooter on the docks, alongside the main road into Felixstowe.

We paid the ships' mate and set off. When we got to Harwich, we asked "When's the next ferry back mate?" The man said "There in't no more today pal. This is the last one on a Sunday, like!" We were fools not to ask beforehand, *but* he had seen us leave the scooter and get on, so we thought he was a fool too. There we were, stuck in Harwich on a Sunday evening with everywhere closed and nothing to do. Not even a Café to quench our thirst or hunger was open. We did find a small shop on the outskirts though and bought some snacks and a bottle of Pop: best we could do with a very, very long walk ahead of us! This little adventure had us walking pretty much all the way from Harwich to Ipswich, with no busses or trains, nowhere open to get food or drink. That's a 32 mile journey if you take the little used B Roads and not the main A12! In Ipswich we eventually managed to find a bus that took us out towards the Felixstowe road and gave our feet a well-deserved rest, but that was only on the North-East side of Ipswich and nowhere near our destination. Then we had to walk and hitch a ride to get back to the docks. Eventually, very late at night and worn out, we got back to the docks. There, to my great surprise, the scooter still stood just as we'd left it. Tired and very weary, without food or drink since Sunday lunch-time (a cuppa and a roll!) we headed back to Great Yarmouth, eventually getting home in the "wee hours" of early morning. That was my last trip to either Felixstowe or Harwich on a scooter!

One of the joys of owning a scooter in those days was that petrol was cheap then, around 10/- (.50p) for a tank full, *with* a few shots of Two-Stroke Oil at around 1d (a Penny) a shot! Lambretta fuel tanks usually hold just under two gallons (no, I'm not looking up Litres!): if you really want Decimal let's say 1.7 Gallons. On that tank-full you could average about 130 miles or so, depending on speed, hills, etc. Going to Leicester was possible on a full tank, then topping up on the outskirts when I got there, or before the return journey.

Just for the Buzz.

Trips around the Norfolk countryside were far more frequent. As you can imagine, the country roads were a lot quieter then, so you could enjoy a good amble around bramble, stop for a puff in the rough, enjoy the breeze under the trees. Pubs in those days were not open all day, so if you fancied a bit of liquid refreshment you either had to take water with you, or wait until opening time at 6pm. Not all country pubs were friendly to Mods, or Rockers come to that, as many locals feared an invasion or fight, after reading the trash in the rags, and gave such youths hostile looks. Being a Mod and sitting in a country pub was a bit like being in a Hitchcock scene! On several occasions I recall going into pubs and being told "We don't want no trouble in 'ere!" by some grizzled barman. Heaven help you if you joked about it too, like I did... (Looking casually over shoulder) "Oh, expecting some are we?" or "Well, please don't start any then!" Easy way to get refused service or make locals grunt with disapproval.

It was nice on a summer's day, if you just finished work at 2 p.m. or 5 p.m. to go for a spin around some of the country lanes. On one such jaunt I recall a bee landing on my Parker. It was a quiet lane, I was going slowly and trying to coax the bee onto my left hand. Being more concerned about the bee, I wasn't really looking where I was going, so hit the far-side curb, or bank, and when I tried to correct the steering got thrown off. First thing I did was check to make sure I hadn't squashed the bee, but he'd gone. What a fool I felt!

Apparitions.

Caister-on-Sea had many more back lanes then than it does now, as the by-pass used up much of the then unused space between farms. It was during the sixties that we moved to Caister-on-Sea due to my father's ill health. We had a bungalow in Saxon Gardens, sometimes visited late at night by Saxon Ghosts. No kidding. There was a Saxon burial ground nearby and the old Roman Shore Fort too. Where our bungalow stood there had been a pathway through that plot, so I discovered in the early hours of one morning, when the Siamese Cat alerted me too it. I was visited by a Saxon man one night too: 2 am he woke me up from a deep sleep, saying telepathically "Look to the bottom of the bed." Dead ghosty git, you woke me up!

Fisher Boys.

It was an unsettled time in 1965 to 1966 but we still managed to live life pretty much to the full. To some extent the streets were hostile, with a few throwback Teddy Boys, the odd Rocker who liked to fight anyone, plus the Lowestoft Fisher Boys, who had a very bad reputation for fighting dirty, with razor blades sewn into their lapels, or carrying cut-throat razors. Always in large gangs so as to increase their chances of winning against one or two unsuspecting strangers. Cowardly behaviour.

Youz Feckin Hard Jimmy?

This brings back a later memory, from round about late summer or autumn 1966/7 (I think?) After spending a night in the Park Tavern with my mates, Tony & Ricky (brothers), we diverted our game of darts to take my then girl friend to the bus stop in the town centre, King Street to be precise. Putting her on the last Eastern Counties bus, about 10:30 pm, we headed back to the tavern to resume darts and beer drinking. On the way past the junction of Regent Road and park Road we encountered a bunch of about 12 or 13 Scottish "Fisher Boys" heading the other way toward Regent Road and on the other side of the street, nearing The Bloater Shop. They were chanting, shouting and generally being pissed and aggressive, like they did. Fights between Scottish and Lowestoft fishermen were common and they used some really low tricks, like Cut Throat Razors, Flick Knives and razor blades sewn into the rims of their hats, lapels, boots and sleeves where any one might grab or be prone to a kick or head butt! As we got to the Park Road entrance, Tony and Ricky said "Sod this!" and were off as quick as a greyhound. Muggings here said, "What's the worry, they're not after us?" and continued to walk towards the park.

Next thing I knew this one man had peeled off from the group and swiftly caught up with me. Approaching me from the left side, just as I was level with the first house's driveway on Park Road, he asked, "Are you f**kin' hard jimmy!" I looked at him in idle curiosity, wondering why someone would ask such stupid question. Then I looked over my shoulder and saw the formation following him and heading in my direction, heads forward in focus. I replied something like, "Thirteen to one, are you kidding?!" Next thing, before I had time to think, a lightning fast head butt struck my head from the left side. He was well practiced. The blow sent me reeling to my right, knocking me into the first driveway. As I started to recover more flurries of physical assault started to rain on me and I found myself surrounded by four, then five, six and more Scottish fisher boys until they had all run across the road to join in. No time to think. Try to stand up and guard against the raining blows. This was before I started formal training in Martial Arts unfortunately; otherwise I may have had some better responses, although at the time I did pretty well, never having faced such odds before.

The raining blows sent me down five or six times, but four or five times I got up, quickly, as you do, and tried to fend off these ignorant louts as best as possible, with the odd punch here and there. On the fifth wave of assault I remember seeing the guy who started it all was on my left side. I was almost half way up the house path, a crazy-paved pathway beside a drive. In front of me were four men intent on trying to hit me and on my right another one who seemed to be preparing for a head-butt or whatever. Behind the men in front of me were others who were trying to reach past them and punch me, determined to get their share of the prize to brag about, but they were blocking each other's way: to my advantage. It was one of those slow-motion moments. My mind took note of the "head-butt man" who started the affray on my left, standing and drawing back his horizontal fist to punch me in the kidney area, the man directly in front who had his legs parted because he was trying to maintain balance as those behind pushed and jostled and the man to my right who was about to bring his head forwards in a habitual head-butt. In an instant I had drawn my loose darts from my saggy left pocket of my old leather coat, these I stabbed into the back of the hand of the man who began the fight with me. At the same time the man in front with legs asunder received a kick in the groin from my right foot and the man at the right side who was attempting head-butting me got a swift punch on the nose as he lurched forward. My last observation was of an eager and tiger-eyed man at the back, trying to get to me past his mates shoulders at the front. This caused a shock wave reaction that made everyone lurch forward into me, or one punched me. Unfortunately at the time I was standing on only one leg, my left leg, and the action sent me spiraling off-balance and to the ground clockwise. Down for the sixth time.

It appears I hit my right temple on the crazy paving as I fell then blacked out with immediate effect. Waking up in hospital A&E, not far away in King Street, I was bemused. My memory had temporarily gone: amnesia was discovered by me for the first time in my life…. As far as I know and some of it was never recovered. Before me as I came round was a man in a green collared coat who for some reason, not comprehended by me at the time, was saying. "Can you hear me? Do you know where you are?" There were two young lads standing there too. This is obviously a strange sight to wake up to, so makes you even less coherent about what is happening. Eventually and succinctly, my reply was "No. Who the hell are you and where am I?" Apparently two young lads about twelve to fourteen years old had found me, comatose, in the driveway. They said they had seen the fisher boys run off shouting, they then supported me both sides and I had (apparently) walked with them to hospital. This I have never recalled. It took me several hours before I could remember my name, let alone the full events of that night. My so-called "mates" never came near me for weeks and I had forgotten them anyway, and my girl friend of the time, completely abandoned me also, and never attempted to contact me! Nobody came to see me at home. Nobody called. There's an old saying, "With friends like that who needs enemies?" but I spawned my own version, "With friends like that who needs an enema?" Literally, my life was blank. I did not know what happened, where I used to hang-out or who my mates were. Losing your memory is a scary thing. It leaves you in a void, with no identity or direction. This, I suppose, must be a bit like Dementure with older people. Bless them, it must be awful and so frustrating, knowing that you had friends and family but not remembering names or details.

It was over a fortnight before I remembered Tony and Ricky, and that was only because my Dad had asked about them/or they had asked him about me. Again, I can't recall much as I had Amnesia, but I suppose my parents gradually tried to help me piece things together. For months I tried to remember but got confused, thinking it had been a fight with a bunch of Rockers! It's quite awful not knowing who you are, who or where your friends are or even where you have been.
Apparently, the girlfriend at the time thought I had dumped her, so didn't even check to see if I had or if I was still alive! That's

nice. Later, much later, one of my friends mentioned her and I vaguely remembered a bit more of that awful night's events, but someone said that she was already seeing someone else, so that put an end to that, and as she wasn't even bothered about finding out what had happened to me... on we get with life. Only in 2017 did I speak to an old Mod pal, 'Churchie', who said that he was standing by the Regal at the time and saw me heading towards the Scottish Fisher boys. He saw Tony and Ricky leave hastily too and also left the scene. Just for the record, no grudges lads as not everyone is as keen as me to stand up for themselves and I really didn't think they'd be so cowardly as to attack one, two or three innocent people.

Amnesia – The Void. For a very long time my memory suffered. It was only when walking around the town that I would bump into people who knew me. Sometimes their faces were familiar, other times not. When they started talking to me though I'd remember them as a friend and we just kind of continued life as you do, one day at a time. It was probably that event which made my memory very patchy, as well as "empty" for certain things. Hence, in writing this book I have had to ask many old friends about events of those times, what year, where or with whom it was all taking place. It's really weird having such a good time in the 60's yet not remembering the basic things, like names and dates! This past couple of years – 2015 to 2018 – have been a real eye-opener for me. Thank you again for all my old chums who have helped me piece that period together. For this book I had to make a Spreadsheet with years and seasonal sections on that I could fill in with events, as and when they came to light.

Who?

As mentioned earlier, it was during '66 that I worked at Bird's Eye, on the Swedish Tunnel, "re hydrating" peas (adding a layer of ice!), then getting across the river for band practice. That was at the school near The Chalet. Who? I Mentioned 'The Who'. They performed at The Tower Ballroom in 1966. To quote a story in the local paper by Mod Colin Stanley "Colin Stanley saw The Who at the Tower Ballroom when they appeared on 23 March 1966. He remembers Roger Daltrey banged the cymbal and cut his hand on the side and all the girls threw handkerchiefs up on the stage. He picked some up and wiped his hand on them and threw them back into the audience. They were fighting over these handkerchiefs." While I didn't recall that bit of the evening I did see my old pal Muggy Driver who was one of the "Bouncers" that night. Being a big bloke, he was charged with keeping girls back off the stage, if they got too close. However, the lead singer Roger Daltrey, kept taking something small out of his shirt pocket and appearing to swallow them/it (numerous times!). His singing got livelier and he pulled back the Mic stand and let it go. It rocked so hard that it fell off stage. Muggy, who was close, picked it up, plonked it back on stage and gave Daltrey a bit of a look. That made me laugh, because if you knew Muggy like I knew Muggy, that "look" meant he wasn't amused. Daltrey almost immediately pulled it back and let it go again, and again rocking off-stage. Muggy went back, picked it up, slammed it back in front of Daltrey's feet and gave him a really pissed-off look. Roger Daltrey immediately tried to pull it back again, but Muggy held on to it with ease as he glared at Roger Daltrey. Oh how I laughed at that little episode. Daltrey managed to keep the stand on stage for the rest of the gig.

Muggy (R.I.P.) was a very big chap. I can remember when I was about 16 or so, walking with him and four others from the Pleasure Beach. Two of the group were boyfriend and girlfriend. They were having a silly argument about something and it got louder. Both were wearing leather jackets and denim jeans. It was a nice day and we were right by the boating lake, next to the Pleasure Beach. Muggy said "Shut up arguing you two prats!" but they carried on arguing. Muggy picked up one in each hand, by their collars, and as he dangled them over the water said "I can't f*****g stand to hear people argue!" and dropped them in the water. That shut them up and we all had a good laugh about it later.

One time later, about 1968, I think, when I had a Mini Van, I saw Muggy walk out onto Nelson Road. He worked in a garage near the Northgate Hospital and had just finished work. I was heading towards the town, so pulled up. "Hey Muggy. Want lift mate?" He turned and had to crouch to look into the van. "Hello Mick. Yes mate, if you're going my way. Wouldn't want to put you to any trouble." He was a very considerate man, but most people only credited him with fighting. "No trouble Muggy. I am going your way." With that he opened the door and slid his huge frame into the Mini's passenger seat. The van very quickly tilted to the left, about 30 degrees! I could hardly reach the gears and the engine was audibly straining to haul us along. Like I said, Muggy was a big bloke. Bless him. Many people feared him because he was as hard as the proverbial nails, but I liked him because he was also honest, down-to-earth and a very self-assured and a fair man too.

There were a few "characters" in Great Yarmouth at the time who all got mislabelled by people who feared them, or who didn't understand them, but several were my pals, like Vicky Turner, the only lad in GY who was called "half-cast" or "black". Poor old Vicky had to fight every inch of the way in his life against bigots, racists and plain ignorant fools. Yes, he did get into trouble, but that was just circumstances. At heart he was a good lad. Coming from Cobholm Island didn't help either as many people looked down on the place. One of my good mates, Mike Poxon, comes from Cobholm and he is one of the most intelligent people I have ever met, speaking Latin, as well as other languages, and very knowledgeable in Astronomy, Computer Programming and other subjects that are far beyond me. Never judge a book by its cover. In my whole life so far, I have met many, many people, some nice, some nasty. With all honesty I can say that the people who appear to come from richer or more highly educated backgrounds are some of the worst people with the most prejudices and worst minds I've ever come across. Not all, but quite a few. My experiences have shown me that many from these so-called "upper classes of society" are the most likely to become perverts, perverts in law, or power freaks who ultimately damage the fabric of society. Whilst the so-called "lower classes" and "working classes" are in fact truly the "salt of the earth".

While we are talking about characters, do any of our readers of the era remember a tramp they used to call "Snowy"? He was about 5' 8", had long wavy white hair and a full wavy beard too. He was always very clean and fairly well dressed. My father was talking to a colleague one day when Snowy was mentioned. My father was amazed to find out who he was, so visited him where he stayed, in a shed over Cobholm Allotments. Snowy used to be a Rolls Royce Engineer. He had vast knowledge of engineering and motor mechanics, but got to a point, like many do, when he said "Enough!" and walked away from his well-paid job, even family and friends. He left the system. Yes, it never pays to take people by face-value.

Leicester – 147 Miles.
It was also in 1965 that I went to Leicester for a break. Having met some Leicester city scooter boys in Great Yarmouth, I decided, for whatever reason, that I would take a trip to visit them. Early one morning I set off on my Lambretta to make the 147 mile trip. It was indeed a slow and monotonous trip, the

mono-tone being the constant drone of the little engine, pushing me forwards at around 50-60 mph: until you came to a hill, then it was a gradual slow down, change from third gear to second, sometimes down to first gear to make it to the top of the hill. There used to be a very long and steep hill on the approach to Leicester, about 10 or 12 miles out. Once you reached the top, if the air was clear of fog and mist, you could just about make out the city in the distance. If you have never ridden a motorbike or scooter that far, let me tell you, it's a bum numbing experience you'll never forget! Seeing your destination in sight is a relief, but not as much a relief as getting off the saddle, like a bow-legged weary cowboy. There were no motorways or motorway services then, so you just kept going. This was a trip I did several times, in sunshine, rain, fog, you name it!

On reaching Leicester I somehow met up with three of the local scooter boys. One of them said I could go back to his family home. All I can recall now is that it was a semi-detached house. No idea where exactly, but it was a Council House on a wide main road. Four scooters in total roared back to his place just after darkness fell. His mum was very welcoming, as were his sisters and brother, one girl who was 18 the other about 14 and little brother about 9. We had tea and I was graciously offered the couch for the night at the end of the evening. His mates left. Mum took the young ones off to bed and I was left in the darkened room by myself, well, that was the plan. Lights out and off up the wooden hill they all went. But then, the older girl came back quietly into the room and plonked herself on the arm of the chair with her legs across my lap, put her arm around my neck and started talking to me and then kissed me quite enthusiastically. She was very attractive, with long dark wavy hair and a nice figure too. She told me she loved Mods and wanted to be with me a bit longer. Who was I to refuse such an attractive girl? Time passed and she kissed me almost furiously: I believe I should say "passionately"?! Well, I have to be honest. At that time I was only 19 and knew pretty much nothing about girls whatsoever. I was only 17 when I had my first sex and that was probably so pathetic that neither of us could remember it later. Here I was, with this gorgeous girl, now sitting on the arm of the chair, snogging me like crazy. After about five minutes or more she lifted my right hand from her waist and placed it on the inside of her thigh. Was I bold? No. Was she? Yes. Was I nervous? Yes! She opened her legs a bit and lifted my hand, encouraging me to explore further, so I did. To my horror and amazement I discovered that her knickers were soaking wet! What?! Never had I encountered this before: after all, I was still young and innocent and not at all enlightened about women's anatomical or physical events. I really thought that she had peed her pants or something and didn't know what to do. Sadly, in retrospect, I made excuses and said I was tired and had to sleep. After that long journey I was tired, it had been a tediously slow journey at speeds of 50 to 60 odd mph, and of course 30 through many built-up areas not by-passed then

Poor girl. What an ignorant young fool I was. In my defence though I have always been naive and probably a big disappointment to many gorgeous young women who wanted to bed me but never got the chance because I just don't get the "signals" (and to be honest still don't! Having said that, I have always been a bit fussy too, so turned down quite a few gorgeous girls just because I felt no "spark". Oh well!) To be fair, there were many young men like me who found that although women were more outgoing, they would stop short of making it too obvious in fear of being called a tart or whatever. Many regrets of growing up without a sex education like they get today at schools: not that it seems to do much good.

Mods & Rockers.

There were not any *real* fights. On one occasion though Sonia and I were at the front of a huge group of Mods that were gathered at the Britannia Pier, going towards the Pleasure Beach. That was because a solitary little fella kept running back and forth between the Mods and the Rockers, saying that the "other lot" were coming and there was going to be a big fight. Little did we realise at the time, and as I later found out, that this thoroughly undesirable little chappie was working for the local Press, who wanted a big story for their grubby little parochial paper, the Yarmouth Mercury (a.k.a. Tomorrow's chip wrapper!) When we got to The Jetty, the newspaper photographers were waiting and the police rolled up in large numbers wielding truncheons and screaming. As some Mods or Rockers were carrying weapons, everybody ran onto the beach to drop them discreetly, the Rockers ran back towards the Pleasure Beach and us lot back towards the Britannia Pier! Nobody got hurt, nobody got caught with weapons that I knew of, and though I think the police grabbed a couple of stragglers and arrested them for "causing a disturbance": what a farce, just an easy way to get more money out of people to pay the law workers.

The real culprits got away with it, and that was the Press! Still, we all had a laugh about it and just carried on with our day. If the truth is told, I think it was a bit of a game more than anything else. The police liked to harass young people, so the young people treated it like a game of cat and mouse. It was entertainment, not violence, as the shite hawks portrayed it.

The Anglo Café.

Situated between Middle market Road and South Market Road, the Anglo was a handy café for the town centre, but more so for a large car park just opposite. In late '65 to '66 I used it a lot. The owner, Leo, used to make an excellent mug of tea and used those nice crusty rolls for his cheese and tomato rolls (Baps, if you're from t' midlands). I can recall that one day, probably a Saturday or Sunday, I sat in The Chalet Coffee Bar, on the right, just as you go in the door. It was quiet. A couple of mates came in as I was finishing whatever I'd had. We started chatting. One of them then said "Here Lucky. You like the Anglo don't you?" So I said I did. "The Rockers have taken it over. We can't go ion there again!" In a state of dismay or uncertainty, I thought "Sod that for a lark!" at the thought of not getting one of Leo's prize teas again and headed back to Great Yarmouth.

As I entered South Market Road and the car park, I saw six motorcycles parked randomly across the whole car park. I paused at the entrance, surveyed the scene and took note that the dead centre of the car park was between three of the machines, a Norton, AJS and a BSA. With my lovely Lambretta parked up between them, claiming the centre, I strolled into the café. Leo was behind the little counter. The conversation went something like:
"Leo!"
"Oh… ahh, Mr Lucky! (Pause) What you want?"
"One of your lovely mugs of tea and a cheese & tomato roll please Leo."
"Oh… is not such a good idea."
"Yes it is Leo. I'm starving mate!"
(I put money on the counter. He shrugged and took it.)
"I don't want a no trouble in here."
"Trouble? I'm here to eat, not cause trouble Leo. You know me!"
With that he made the tea and handed me the roll. I went through to the main area where two Rockers sat on the right-hand side, another two near the front door and one closer to

the back. I sat at the middle table of four on the left side, then began eating. I kept my Parka on, even though I had my ¾ leather coat underneath and my Moleskin trousers. All was quiet for around twenty minutes. As I finished my roll and was about to make a roll-up to smoke, a voice suddenly got louder from opposite my table. "'Ere, you're a fucking Mod ain't you?!" I casually looked towards the leather clad young man and thought that his powers of deduction were totally amazing.
"Yes." I replied, "And you're a Rocker."
He looked down at his attire…
"Yes!"
I held my hands out in that famous French gesture…
"So. What about it?"
He looked bemused and returned to chatting with his mate. Nobody else said anything. Half-an-hour later I left, thanked Leo and mounted my scooter, which was in fine fettle.
For some weeks and months to come I continued to go in The Anglo Café and enjoy Leo's fine Teas & Rolls. On a Saturday night the place was packed, but I had a table all to myself, and no matter how many Rockers and their girlfriends were standing, nobody seemed to want to share my table.

One Saturday evening, in the summer, it was packed, as usual. There I sat in my full Mod regalia, also as usual. The back door was flung open and I heard a cry of "Rockers are fucking wankers!" come from that way. Everybody stopped, looked around. There were a bunch of about a dozen Norwich Mods shouting abuse. The Rockers started heading towards the back door and the Norwich Mods ran down the street as fast as their legs could carry them. Still sitting at my table I thought "Oh no, this could be embarrassing, hopefully not downright nasty!"

A few minutes later the Rockers all poured back into the café amongst excited comments about how they'd chased the Mods down to the seafront. One of the Rockers, a regular, loudly proclaimed "Yeah, them Mods are fuckin' wankers in'they!" Then realised a Mod was sitting in the cafe. He turned towards me and said "Sorry, not you mate, no offence!"

I laughed and said "None taken." They were Norwich Mods and if they were the ones who kept nicking things off our scooters, then it's a pity they didn't catch them!

As it happens, one of the Rockers who was in there one night was an old friend. Dave, I think the man's name was, a tall blonde-haired young man, clean shaven and not too "greasy". He was one of the first to buy a Japanese Super-bike in Great Yarmouth: and I had a ride on that one night over in Gorleston; that's another story. He recognised me immediately when another bright sparked chirped up "Here, there's a f**kin' Mod in 'ere!" The café silenced. Must admit, I did think I was going to be in a brawl that time and slightly outnumbered by about 30-1. There were several occasions when I was sat or stood next to a Rocker and said "So what?!" when they noticed I was a Mod. Neither did I care nor was I frightened. They were just ordinary people like us, but rode larger two-wheeled vehicles. Most of them were decent lads too. There were the odd ones who were a bit, shall we say "Nuttier" than the rest. That's life. End of.

Our pal Richard Leavold, one of the Anglo Rockers, has this picture on his fantastic website (previous page):

https://great-yarmouth-modsrockers.weebly.com/rockers-gallery.html

Chapter Four.

1966.

Like I said, 1966 was a busy old year and I can't remember all of it. Being young I was busy working, and when I wasn't working I was finding my feet, discovering the joys and the sorrows of the opposite sex, maintaining a vehicle (just as unreliable!), hanging around in coffee bars, etcetera, and going out with my many friends and having fun. Riding the scooter wasn't every day. There were times when it was better to leave it at home. The summer of '65 and '66 were such times. Many Mods came to Gt. Yarmouth from London, Southend, Grimsby, Sheffield, and Manchester and all over the country. A lowly few would be nicking bits off our scooters. Whatever, it was best to keep the scooters we cherished safely tucked out of the way. For quite some time we used a car park tucked awy just off the top of Regent Road.
(See picture below)

Our out of the way car park, behind what was The Bloater Shop.

Hello, Hello, Hello.
One place we used to park was a small car park just tucked away behind 'The Bloater Shop', atop of Regent Road, near the park. We had talked to the residents, whose houses backed onto the car park and they were quite happy for us to be

there, as long as we kept the noise to a minimum. This we did. Sitting there having a chat one day, one of my mates said he wanted to go somewhere nearby. Offering him a lift on the pillion, we set off up the road. Now, I say "up" the road, but it was a One Way road which was "down" towards Nelson Road Central! It was hardly ever used by cars and we rarely saw a car come by. Traffic was a lot thinner in those days. Just as we set off, staying close the left pavement, a burly Police Sergeant comes walking around the corner. He immediately held up his left hand in the "Stop!" position, and I stopped.

The conversation went something like this:
"Hello, hello, hello... (I'm kidding!) Stop! You know it's an offence to travel the wrong way along a one way street?"
"Yes, I was only going one w..."
"If a car came around that corner it would likely hit you and you'd cause a nasty accident..." etcetera. He then got his notebook out and started to take details.
"Name?" he asked.
When I told him, he asked my address. When I told him that his attitude changed dramatically. "Any relation to Siddy Symonds who runs ECMEC garage?"
"Yes. My dad."
His attitude changed like the wind! "Oh, well, I know your father well. Very nice man. He'd be so upset if you had an accident and got hurt." With which he tucked his notebook back into his tunic pocket and smiled... well, almost. He then told me that my father was a very nice man and that he knew him from the Masonic Club. Followed by "When you see your dad tell him that Sergeant ****** sends his best regards. Now you take it steady young man. Hang on." He then held up his hand for us to remain there, stepped back a few paces into the middle of the road, held up his left hand for any traffic coming from Regent Road area to stop or give way, then ushered me

out of the road, still going the wrong way!

My mate had been nudging me in the back while all the two-faced conversation had been going on. As we sped off he said "What the f*** was that all about. What a ****!" said my mate.

"Yes", I said . Sergeants upwards can join the Masonic. He's doing a bit of licking." When I got home and saw my Dad that night, I told him about the incident. He just gave a little laugh and said "Yes. I'll probably see him at the weekend. He's about due for a new car." It was in those formative days that I learned about corrupt police, corrupt judging and the bending of the law to suite those who worked in their "gang" or the rich sicko's that support them. The "establishment" are about as honest as Ali Baba but with far more than Forty Thieves. Corruption and abuse of power, from the government down.

In A Flash!

On educational incident was after I had just finished doing up my scooter after *another* crash. My father, bless him, had straightened it all out and repaired it again. Never did he moan or scold me. I think he was just happy that I wasn't on a faster motorbike and was still alive after all. This time I had painted it up, added a clip-on new Front Carrier, a 6v VW Horn and other bits. It had taken over two weeks to get sorted, so I was full of joy to get it back on the road again. I took a picture of it for the first and only time. With not much fuel in the tank I set off for Regent Road and the Seafront. A large group of the lads and lasses were gathered down Regent Road. They all said how great the scooter looked. One of my pals at that time, Barry Pigano, said "Aw, take me for ride on it Lucky!" I said I hadn't got much money or petrol, so couldn't go far. He said "That's OK mate, I'll give you ten bob towards juice if you give me a pillion down the seafront!" So, with an offer of petrol that couldn't be refused, off we went.

It was a glorious summer's day around June/July. I had just finished doing up the scooter again, after a previous crash. It looked so good with the new Front Carrier and fresh paint job

(see inset picture left). The seafront was heaving with traffic, two lanes full each way. There were two identical Austin Westminster cars in the left-hand lane, just in front of us. As we reached Trafalgar Green, I heard a voice shout "Lucky!" Instinctively I glanced around but then realized I needed to be looking at the road ahead. As I quickly turned back the driver of the second of the two Austin Westminster's had decided he wanted to turn into Trafalgar Road, so swerved in front of me putting his indicator on at the same time. Literally this happened in no more than two seconds. I instantly decelerated and tried swerving to the left, or centre of the two lanes, but he was braking hard as well. All in an instant I had looked over my left shoulder, attempted to brake, swerve and avoid the car, but to no avail. One of those slow motion moments happened next.

I saw a slow-motion explosion of clear glass and red and amber plastic as I lurched forward and the scooter hit his rear nearside light assembly. There was a flash of silver as the chromed front carrier shot upwards. Then as the amber, red and white glass slowly fanned outwards and upwards I lurched back, then forward again and started to fall sideways. However, I couldn't fall off the scooter as both my hands were trapped by the clutch and brake levers which had pushed into the back of the car. No way did I want to fall sideways either, as I may have been hit by traffic coming up behind us, so I decided to twist rightwards and lay across the scooter. As I went down I wondered what had happened to Barry, as he was no longer on the pillion. Just for a fraction of a second I looked back and saw him landing on his back in the road, the chrome front carrier landing on his chest, to add to his already shocked looking face! I was then "bounced" back face-down across the scooter's floorboards, most shockingly. The result? I was carted off to hospital where I had my dislocated shoulder put back and treated, plus both my hands bandaged as they were fractured, the left worse than the right, then had my left arm put in a Sling and told not to take it off for a month or so. Barry was in far better shape. Just shocked and bruised. The scooter… well, my father just asked how I was, then quietly arranged for the scooter to be picked up, put in the garage where he sorted it out yet again. What an absolute star of a man! The sad upshot was that I got fined for "careless driving" when the driver who cut in front of me got away Scott free. Guess why? He was a Clerk to The Magistrates, I was just a youth, a Mod, so who gets the blame? Not the person who works within the legal system, that's for sure.

That was a horrible enough day as it was, but the day got worse. There was a skinny lad from South Yorkshire staying in Great Yarmouth at the time. We called him "Mad John". He was skinny, had a bent nose, kind of unevenly shaped face (sorry fella) and had had a somewhat sheltered upbringing, but was not without money. As he was prone to bullying, and I was always a champion to the cause for the weaker person, I had put him under my watchful and protective wing. *Before this incident*: One day he asked me to accompany him to Norwich on the train. He had ordered and paid for a brand new Lambretta GT200 from the shop on Upper King Street. Off we went on the train and back we came on the scooter, after a hair raising ride as, fresh out of the showroom, John rode us to the top of a hill, by Riverside Road, then back downhill to Riverside at speed, so fast that it almost gave me nightmares!

John loved his scooter and I had warned him not to go too fast on it. When I came back from the hospital with Barry, after the seafront crash, we went to our car park behind the Bloater Shop. My left arm was in a Sling because my shoulder had been dislocated and then sprung back in again. Both my hands were bandaged up as they were damaged by being trapped on the scooter's handlebars. Some of the lads asked me if I was alright and I told them that I was damaged but more pissed-off about my scooter than anything. Then I saw Mad John's scooter screaming around the bend from upper Regent Road into Park Road, he barely missed the entrance to the park by more than a couple of inches, sparks coming off the underside of his machine. When I asked why, one of the lads told me that a certain person (still in the car park) had been bullying him and winding him up, to the point that he almost cried, then rode off on his scooter to vent his frustrations. The person who was responsible was *laughing* about it, bragging to two or three other lads about his bullying a weaker lad. What happened next is not anything that I'm proud of or wish to discuss. He *was* a friend, up until then. His actions unleashed the beast in me to such a degree that my Mind tried to block the event out for many years, even forgetting who it was: in fact if my old mate "Harry" hadn't have told me, I'd still not know now. It's something that I am quite sad about.

Such things should never happen. John eventually saw me, with my arm back in the sling, and slowly calmed down. I took him for a cup of tea and needed one myself, after the day I'd had! Nobody ever bullied John again, and not long later he thanked me for being his friend and went back to his family, somewhere in Yorkshire or Lincolnshire, if I recall correctly: his family who he had never wanted to talk about before. Perhaps he'd been abused. Who knows.

Mad John, as he got nicknamed, left Great Yarmouth after that incident,probably went back home. He was a good lad and wouldn't have said boo to a goose. At least I hope he went home or got to wherever he left for safely.

JOIN THE "JET-SET"
LET YOURSELF GO ON A Lambretta

It was soon late 1966 and the Mod scene started to wilt a bit. Some of the lads went their own way and many started getting cars, selling up their scooters. Minis were popular, so were MG Sports cars. In the meantime though, those younger lads of 15-16 or so that had seen us enjoying the Mod scene, were becoming old

enough to buy scooters. They reached 17, bought scooters and carried on the Mod tradition, but in a much quieter way than we did. The Chalet was still the main venue where Mods met up, and still is today. Pat Weller was one of the younger lads. He was a bit too young when the Mod scene first started, so couldn't have a scooter legally. He soon made up for it later though. Nowadays Pat is the "Font of all knowledge" and he has contributed greatly to revising my memories for this little book. Thank you Pat. Many of the other lads have helped with reviving memories too, Bryan Bream and his "spoon", John, the two Graham's and more.

The Big Dipper!

One day, in The Chalet, I asked Pat for a story relating to those heady times. Here it is abbreviated:

"One night two eighteen year old girls, X and Z, had requested us to go out to the farm, where they were baby-sitting. I went on the back of Lucky's scooter." Recalls Pat. "When we got there, there was this big dip where the vehicles had to wash their wheels when coming onto the farm. Lucky shouted 'feet up' but I couldn't get my feet up in time, we went through it and there was a huge splash! My trousers got soaked. When we got in, the girls were waiting for us. Z said to me "Oh your trousers are soaked. Come through to the bedroom and take them off." Lucky stayed in the living room with X." He added, "I was 14 at the time": obviously she didn't care! Nobody thought about age back then, but overall, it seems that many older girls went out with younger boys, and girls were *much* more forward then.

As the summer of '66 came to an end, the scooter days seem to fade away into a hazy past. The year that had started with a bang went out with a fizzle. At least for me. Problems with a girlfriend meant that it was time to step back, have a break and enjoy a different perspective.

The Mods Boomed!

It was in 1966 that I had my only picture taken of me in Mod gear. That was taken by someone looking over the top of the old open air swimming pool. I could see myself only by the fact that I remembered my "bad taste" period, when checks came into fashion, and my wavy hair. I had on a light coloured jacket, with a feint check pattern, a checked shirt and light coloured trousers with a feint check pattern too, plus brown Chelsea Boots. My hair was collar length and very curly. There I was, centre front, looking over my shoulder to see who a young copper was shouting at. It wasn't me that he was shouting at. By the way, I realised after a week that too much check looked ridiculous, so changed style, yet again: as we did in Mod days. Fashions came and went at a furious pace and we spent a lot of money on clothes, so we started a "mix and match" trend.

(Photo left – 1966 Seafront crowd.) That's me, centre front, in "full cheque fashion clash" mode, looking over my shoulder to see what the aggressive young copper was shouting about. No idea who took it, but thanks. Just look at how many Mods you can see! Just another arrogant young copper trying to earn his "bully badge" as we called it. Many were, and probably still are, failed bullies at school or in the street, so having a uniform gave them the power to push people around without retaliation... most of the time. That was a surprise turning up on the Net!

The 'Pink Slip' Trick.

As said elsewhere, we were persecuted by the press and the police. There were a couple of coppers who used this trick: standing out of the way and waiting for the sound of a scooter coming round from the Burton's direction. If they had a Pillion passenger, they'd get flagged down and have their licence checked. You could only carry a Pillion if you had a full licence, or if the pillion rider had one. They got a few and fined them, of course. Our trick was to pass our test, from which you were handed a "pink slip" paper that said you were now entitled to a full licence. We would then find an unlicensed pillion and ride around the block until we got stopped. "Hello, hello, hello. You know it's an offence to carry a pillion... blah blah blah" then asking you to produce your Driving Licence (a small red book type). On seeing that it was "Provisional" his face would light up with glee as he prepared to give you a "ticket". As he started this, we would then say "Oh no!" and dig into another pocket pulling out the Pink Slop. The copper's face would drop like a stone when he realised that he did not have the upper hand after all! We went off and shared it with he crowd, having a good laugh at getting our own back on these prejudiced bullies.

The rest of 1966 was a maelstrom of events, people and new activities. It was in 1966 when what seemed like "all the Mods" came to Great Yarmouth. Quite a few had visited the year before but '66 saw the seafront absolutely packed with Mods, from one end to the other. Again, no idea who took this picture but it was in the public domain. It clearly shows just how many Mods were in just one part of the seafront at any time. Hundreds. Sadly, we felt that we had to either leave our scooters at home or hide them away in a back street somewhere, away from the main action. It wasn't because of the Rockers, oh no, it was the visiting Mods. Some of them were thieving scum and would steal bits of our scooters. It was bad enough having a small bunch from Norwich like that, let alone or "fellow" Mods from London or wherever.

There used to be a dozen Mods came from Norwich and always used to steal parts or bits off our scooters, if they saw them parked alone at night. We really wanted to get our hands on these low-life scum but never did. Strangely, in 2016 I was chatting to some old drinking pals in a local Pub in Norwich, when this old boy came in. He bragged at one point that he was a Rocker, but he and his mates used to dress up as Mods and go steal parts off scooters in Gt. Yarmouth! I did tell him what he was and that he was lucky to still be laughing about it, but past is past and we all move on.

Still Rock 'n' Rolling on.

The band 'Staircase' was still rocking and rolling on. At one time we had Dave "Porky" Pigford (RIP) on Rhythm Guitar and we had a *string* of lead guitarists (see what I did there?), as Lead Guitarists were generally a funny old lot and found it hard to settle in one place. Kev "Milord" Claxton (now in Jaques de Ladd) came in with us later on, and that brought in some different material, as all musicians have their preferences in musical taste. The summer season at the Sandringham Hotel continued to be our "bread and butter". Then we took on such giddy heights as Caister Youth Club, the Green Gate pub and various party events. We did make it to the Tower Ballroom though, where in the mid 60's the Who played, alongside many other big name local or regional bands. Many of the local bands did a charity gig there and they were well attended and very popular. Sometime later (67/68?) I formed a band called 'Berlin' just for one such charity event there and sang a song I wrote of the same title: basically giving the view that thousands of innocent people also died when Berlin was bombed and that war was two-sides of a coin, not one. Innocent people die in any war torn country. On the same bill were a re-formed Staircase and Kochbacher (it was common for groups to split up and reform under another name, mixing members at the same time. There were so many musicians in Great Yarmouth at that time that bands used to form and split again within weeks, let alone months, so Staircase lasting two years was pretty good. Sadly Staircase didn't last very long after that night, nor did Berlin. In fact I lost interest in singing in 1967/8 as there were too many clashes of characters around.

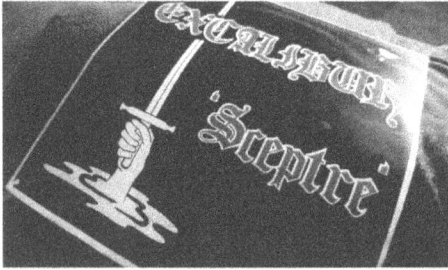

Another one of my musical connections was with a couple of the members of the local band called "Excalibur": Tony Walsh, David Mason, Jim Hewkin and Tom Hewkin. They decided that the big time for them would come if they sank all their money into making a L.P. Record. So they did, at Scratby Recording Studios. I can still visualize the place, in a loft of a Chalet-style house. In fact, I bought one of their LP's, "Sceptre", one of just 99 made – they settled for 99 as the price went too high for them for over 100! The album was so basic that the Jacket was not even glued together, to make a "slot", like normally happens. But it was well pressed vinyl and I still have it, unscathed, sounds perfectly clear too (played twice!).

If you want the URL for tracing 'Music from the East Zone', here it is: www.musicfromtheeastzone.co.uk/bands_artists/EXCALIBUR. htm (Staircase are on the list too.)

1966 was a very busy year indeed. Summertime seemed to last forever in those days, with very few storms. In the exploding world of music there were so many great Bands and solo vocalists coming on the scene that theatres just didn't have to compete; except for the peek week spots.

The Aquarium had much loved Mod band Gerry & The Pacemakers on. I missed that, for whatever reasons. You can see the "family show" aspect by the sheer variety of acts that were on. Perhaps a sign of the times, Billy Fury, with his late 50's style, was squeezed in on the bottom line with Crispian St. Peters, whoever he was! Mack and Kirk? Your guess is as good as mine!

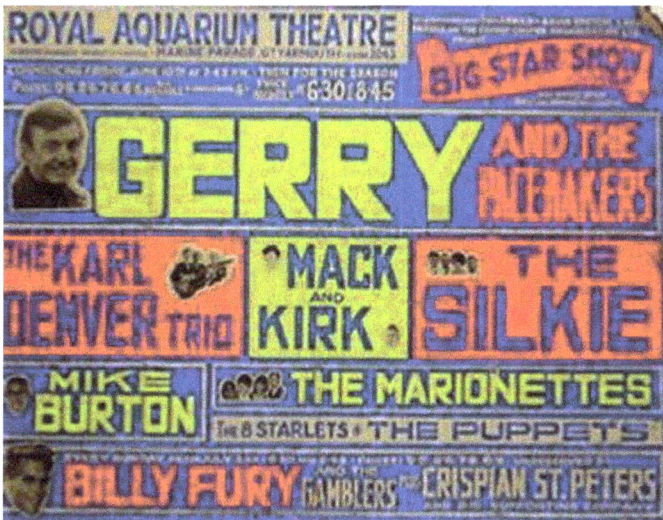

The ABC Regal on the other hand had this little lot for the summer: 'Dave Dee, Dozy, Beaky, Mick & Tich.', 'Paul & Barry Ryan', 'The Koobas', 'Billie Davis', 'The End', 'Rob Storme & The Whispers', with Ray Cameron as Compeer.

Sunday June 26th at the Great Yarmouth 'Britannia Theatre, on the pier, saw 'The Who', 'The Merseys', 'Oscar', 'The Fruit Eating Bear' (!), 'The Herd' and 'Genevieve. That's not even counting the Wellington Pier or the Windmill Theatre! A hot summer indeed. Great Yarmouth was not only packed with talent but packed to the brim with holiday makers, many of whom by that year were teenagers having holidays with their pals. This was not unusual as past generations did similar; e.g. I recall my mother telling me that when she was in her late teens, she and a friend would go to places like the hut at Potter Heigham, on the GY side of the bridge. On a Saturday evening they'd have dances. Young men on holiday from University would hire Cruisers for a holiday and to show off would have the latest in music technology on deck, a wind-up Gramophone! With his they'd go to the local pubs or dances and chat-up the local girls; who then, like now, weren't all easy prey for horny young men, though then, as now, some were just as horny and eager to have fun with these smart young men wearing blazers and 'straw boater' hats! Not much has changed then, except fashions, eh?!

Great Yarmouth was at the head of the Norfolk Broads, literally as the two rivers that run through the beautiful Broads both meet at the southern end of Breydon Waters and become the Yare-mouth.

Readers who shared this era may agree with me when I say "These were the halcyon days!" Just like the generation my mother revelled in, where music like The Charleston and Black Bottom shocked their parents, fashions changed too, we had our "Swinging Sixties" peak in '66. This picture (from the Public Domain) brings back some great memories of the times and fashions. Fashions Like Winds. The fashions were like the winds, changing every few minutes. You could buy something one week and it would be out of date the next. Like the Beatle's suit I bought in 1963, charcoal grey with a black velvet collar, then the next thing you know they start a trend for cutting 3" off the legs! The earlier "two-tone" fashions were soon replaced by Moleskin Trousers, Camel hair Coats and for the women Mary Quant fashions, checks one week, stripes the next, then Pop Art designs. It was hard to keep up with. Some of the crowd would take a trip down to Carnaby Street in London to go look at what was trendy in shops like Lord John's, Lady Jane's and Beyond the pale (Boutique), to name but three.

(Lady Jane's Boutique in Carnaby Street, c.1995 - pic. Public Domain.)

Chapter Five.

1967.

Later on in '67, back home.
At that time I had a steady girlfriend and she wanted me to get a car. Putting my scooter up for sale I got a nice little beige coloured Mini Van. My mates and I had many adventures in that, including one Sunday night we went to the Tower Ballroom. As the new Drinking & Driving Law had just come in I only had a half-pint about 9 pm. Then at 10:30 the Tower shut. We decided to go to Lowestoft to get some fish and chips at a really good shop there. Off we went.

Then, coming back out of Lowestoft about 12:30 pm, we got stopped by a police van. A fresh-faced young PC, who was also rather arrogant, stopped me on the premise that I was cornering fast (I was doing about 20 mph). I explained that part of the front suspension was knackered and that, though parked, it was still "leaning over" slightly. He wasn't having it, even though it was plain to see and wanted to show-off in front of his mates. He then demanded that I take a Breath test. This proved nothing and was in fact "negative" but he then demanded I leave my mates stranded and vehicle parked on the side of the road quite near to Corton. He arrested me, for no good reason, in fact "False reasons". I was taken back in the police van with a gang of leering morons, then locked up in a cell. Insulted by an arrogant old Sergeant who took my details and description, then locked up again until a doctor could arrive to do a blood test. This idiot turned up, swabbed my arm and then stuck a syringe in it to take some blood. He tested it and found it to have "over the limit" amount of alcohol in it! When I asked how this could be, he fobbed me off and aid that I must be a *liar* and that I must have had more than half-a-pint. I was subsequently charged, then released about 9 am the next day to walk back to my van. Later I was banned from driving for one year and fined.

[Note: We now know that those idiots did that to many, many people. They swabbed the arm in a 100% Alcohol Rub before taking the blood. Hence the alcohol from the rub gives a positive reading. Did I ever get a pardon, apology, my money back? No! False conviction.]

It was in 1967 I met "Marty", Martin Slack. Martin was working at the Birds Eye Development building on South Quay. When I first worked there I had my scooter still, but then swapped to four wheels and the Mini Van. Martin, I'm pleased to say, is still one of the regulars at The Chalet. Nowadays he hangs out with Graham Hales and Graham Dallimore and they pursue the gentle art of Bowling. In fact in 2018 Martin won a trophy, first prize for getting his balls in the right place, near someone called Jack, apparently! Seriously though, well done Martin.

One day, when knocking off work, I drove my Mini Van out onto the road and saw this wheel go rolling past me. I thought, "That looks like a mini wheel!" and suddenly the front near-side wheel dropped to the roads, sparks coming off the hub.

1967 – Summer of Love & Peace.
My Minivan had packed up in '67 and I was between cars. I had borrowed my father's Hillman Minx saloon and gone out with Barry, Tony and Ricky. This ended up in a bit of teenage stupidity and the rear window got shattered. By this time my father had already had a heart attack and a mild stroke, so was not too well. As usual, he fixed the window but I had to pay some damages and he did have words with me on that

occasion. One evening a few weeks later I wanted to borrow the car again. My father was a very patient and trusting man. He knew that having done something stupid once that I wouldn't do it again. He gave me the keys. My mother, on the hand, was a nag and had quite a temper on her. She really started having a go at him as I walked out and went to the car. She was insisting that he should take the keys back off me and not allow me to borrow it. That ended up in a regrettable tug-o-war that snapped the keyring in two! That made me feel bad too. That same day Tony and Ricky had a row with their parents. We decided that we should go away and clear the air.

That night we all went home late, packed a few things and decided that we'd meet up after midnight near the G.Y. Bus Depot. I walked from Caister-on-Sea and Tony and Ricky were there, waiting for me as they only lived around the corner. We then decided we would go to Leicester and hitch a lift there. Really? So there we are at 1 am, on the Acle Road, trying to thumb a lift to Leicester. How stupid are we when we are teenagers, eh?! There was barely any cars on the road at that time of the morning. After a wasted hour or so we decided that it would be better to split up. I told Ricky to stay with his big brother and I'd go my way separately. We arranged to meet at the open bus depot in Gravel Street, Leicester, according to an old map I just researched. It was late the next evening, after several lifts and many miles walked that I got there. About 11:45 pm I walked through Leicester to the bus station and climbed aboard a parked double-decker. Tony and Ricky arrived too about half-past-midnight. We swapped tales and then tried to get some sleep on the upstairs deck seats. At about 5 am a local copper came along and checked the busses. He asked us our names, where we were from and asked us to walk along the street with him. When he got to a police phone (Call Box) he checked in and checked us out. He then advised us to steer clear of the "Black Jamaican people in Leicester" as he said they went out with English girls, then got them 'on the game' and kicked them downstairs if they tried to leave. He was very adamant that all black men were rotten bastards and that we should not fall foul of these Jamaican immigrants because he had seen so much trouble from them. He also told us that we should stay clear of the area called Highfields, on the east side, as it was full of trouble, crime, prostitution and drugs.

The next day we went to the Dole (Job Centre) and also found a B&B in the Highfields area, on a busy main road too. It was quite close to the factories, like Hush Puppy and Dunlop. We were told by the landlady that the "foreign families" worked shifts at Hush Puppy. The men would buy a pair of comfortable Hush Puppy shoes and one would wear them for the 6 to 2 shift. Then at 2 pm his male relative would come in for the 2 to 10 shift and they'd swap shoes. This way they'd wear out a new pair of shoes in six months, then get them replaced under warranty! No idea if this was true, but it certainly surprised us as nobody we knew would ever dream of such a thing: and we knew some fairly tricky people. We had a Jamaican family next door. Every night someone would come home from work at 2:15 am and play the same two records over and over again, one Blue Beat and the other Scar beat. It drove us mad, as well as keeping us awake. To this day I cannot stand that music.

We had a great time in Leicester and eventually got an unfurnished fat on Highfields Street (I think the name is right). First floor on the eastern side with a square bay window. I got a job with Newday Furnishings Group in their 'G M Browns – High Class Furniture' shop on High Street, just across from Silver Street. Started off as "tea boy" but then became trained as a Salesman as I got on well with the boss and his son, who also worked there. My first week was helping to get the shop ready for opening and making copious quantities of tea: the manager liking my brews. After cleaning the windows, which had been whited over, me and the son decided we'd have a laugh. We both posed in a window each like Harlequin Dummies in a Tailor's shop. As an unsuspecting person or couple walked by we would suddenly move an arm, or just make a quick move and freeze again. The amount of people we caught by surprise was good fun, and many of them laughed when they realised.

Yardie Boys.

Second or third day in and we were out looking for work. No work so we adjourned to a café somewhere around the city centre. As we sat down with our drinks and snacks, there were three girls sitting at another table, taking great interest in us. We just nodded, waved and said hello. They chatted, giggled, conferred and then waved us to go over and sit with them. So we did. We introduced ourselves and said where we were from. They were Leicester girls. After about twenty minutes the café door opened and in walked three black men. One was about 6' 3", big built and had a scar on his face. The other two were about 6' tall and they all looked like they could handle themselves. The girls turned and said "Hi" to them. The look on Tony's face was priceless as the words of the policeman rattled around his head, about how bad these black boys were. They walked over to the table. I was closest. The big fella with the scar looked at me and said, with a really bad stammer "W-w-what are you d-d-d-d-doin' with our g-g-g-g-girlfriends like?" The girls said that they were just chatting and that *they* [us] were from Great Yarmouth. The big guy looked at me, stammered some more and said "R-r-r-r-r-r-r—really?"
"Yes."
"D-d-d-d-d-do y' know D-d-d—d-d-Dave Williams?"
"Yes" I replied, surprised to hear his name "He's a mate of mine

and we used to go to school together."

The big fella laughed, held out his right hand and then shook all of our hands. They squeezed in around the table and we finished or food and drink. We then all left together and were all going towards Highfields (the place we'd been warned to stay away from), so had to walk along Granby Street, towards the station. I remember the pavement was wide, very wide. We were walking nine abreast. The three guys had a bag of something. The big guy, who was next to me as we were chatting about "Yarmuff boys", held out the bag to me, then Ricky and Tony and said "Here, you like Sherbet?" OK, so we walked and dipped our fingers into the "sherbet" and didn't think anything of it... except that the white powder didn't really taste like sherbet. As this was happening a copper in uniform came towards us and walked on the road to go past, avoiding eye contact altogether. As I watched him I thought that was rather strange. We all parted ways near the station and said we'd meet up later. They told us about a little club in Silver Street called the Ill Rondo. There was also a cellar bar nearby, almost opposite, a modernized place: we used to drink in there a lot but it got quite tedious. Apparently "Yarmuff boys" have a bit of a reputation for fighting, so every time there was a fight someone would shout "Get the Yarmuff boys in!" and we'd be summoned. It has to be said here, that if there is a fight that cannot be avoided then, fair enough, I'll swing with the best of them. But, why fight if you can avoid it and have a nice, relaxing, quiet night out. Tony and Ricky however, did not like the word "fight" under any circumstances, so I had to be more careful around them as it could get messy, so tried to keep them away from trouble if possible.

Love & Peace Man.

It while we were living in Leicester and having a really good time, the Hippies arrived. One Saturday Tony, Ricky and I were walking along Granby Street and every few yards a pretty young woman would come up to us, offer us a flower, a kiss on the cheek sometimes, and say "Love and Peace man." What? We had of course seen a few fashions and trends by this time, but what was this? Women outnumbered men in Leicester about 8-to-1 at that time. Most young men were walking around talking about football while the beautiful young women wanted to be loved. We could hardly believe what we were seeing. As Mods we thought "This is it! The next stage of development."

One day some young woman with flowers in her hair, and a painted cheek, approached us and said there was to be a Hippy gathering in De Montfort Hall Park on the Saturday. Off we went. A Large group of young men and women were sitting around in a large oval on the grass. Strange smells wafted through the air, some incense, and another smell that we didn't really know at the time. A young man around 20 stood up. He wore a headband and a sort of goatskin open jacket and had long wavy hair. He took his turn to read a poem he had written.
"Underwear.
Women's underwear is designed to keep thing up.
Men's underwear is designed to keep things down."
He sat down again and someone handed him a rolled cigarette. The crowd murmured, some giggled, and some just said "Yeahh man!"
We watched, in awe. A couple of uniformed coppers were nearby, but as there was no trouble didn't make a fuss. Like us, they probably didn't know what that stranger smell was that cut through the incense being burned.

Sometime later I was with one of the Leicester lads. He was talking about the Hippies and their lifestyle, fashions and trends. We spoke of many things. The Beatles were then getting into Meditation, India and various substances were indicated in their more psychedelic song tracks. Me and (whatever his name was) headed for Abby Park. It was a beautiful sunny day. Abby Park was formerly part of the grounds of Cardinal Woolsey's house, which stands beside it. He was the man who invented socks and eventually a factory sprung up called Woolsey's Socks that I'm sure he never got too much credit for, being long dead. We sat around or laid around on the grass, chatting away. There were a wide mixture of other people in the park too. My pal got out his roll-up baccy tin and asked me if I smoked. I said yes. He then made an unusual roll-up with not one but three papers stuck together. Then he crumbled in some black stuff after heating it up. "What's that?" I asked. "Dope man." He replied. "You not smoked this before?" I shook my head. As far as I knew dope was something you used on a yacht! "It's great." He said as he finished and lit up. He took a deep drag on it then handed it to me, so I did the same. Almost immediately the world started to take on a different appearance as my senses were transformed. As we smoked he pointed to a park keeper and said "Drug Squad!" then laughed. "What?" I had to ask, as it hadn't occurred to me that we had drugs let alone did I know what a Drug Squad was! He explained that they were "secret police" out to "bust" people for smoking dope: the thought seemed quite ludicrous as the stuff seemed to put you in a good mood and not a criminally insane one. We had some laughs and whiled away a couple of hours in the park talking about various subjects, including Cardinal Woolsey who's house is next door to the park and how he invented socks, as he always suffered from cold feet. It was an educational day, to say the least!

Tony and Ricky mainly stayed home weekend days or did their own thing while I formed a number of new friendships in the city. By night we'd hit the many Jazz Clubs, where people like Kenny Ball, Acker Bilk or many other lesser known artists came in to Jam. There were loads of large Pubs around the city in the sixties that had large function rooms, mostly used for Jazz sessions: often impromptu ones, or "jams" as they're known in the music world. Sometimes we'd go to the Ill Rondo or other local bars and meet-up with various local friends. Good times.

Not far from the Clock Tower was the small Market Place. This I loved, especially on a Saturday. There were many bright and colourful Indian material stalls. The Indain Sari is a work of art, not just a dress. The Indian ladies would deliberate for quite some time about the patterns, colours and mixtures of materials, some gold emboidered. During my time at G M Browns - High Class Furnishers, I'd get asked to stand in for the delivery driver's mate. He was "off sick": in other words, there was a major horse racing even on! The driver was a bit wary of me at first, being young, but we soon got on well and worked hard at delivering furnishings, including double wardrobes that had to be lifted up a ladder, on my back, then carefully inserted through a window: after the frame had been taken out! Some deliveries were made to Indian households. When you walked in there was a lovely smell of spices, but what I noticed most was how much pride they placed in keeping their homes clean. Usually more so than most British people did.

There was the odd hitch with deliveries, but none so bad as one event which has burned itself into my mind. We were driving over a road bridge, somewhere on the outskirts, when a motorcyclist came the other way, overtook the car in front of him as they entered the bridge. As often happens, the motorcyclist misjudged the speeds of both himself and the approaching lorry (us). He collided with the front of the lorry on the driver's side and disappeared underneath. Being a scooterist I was in fear of his life. His bike was a mess, so was he, but not dead. We had to get somone to call an ambulance while we talked to the rider and tried to keep him as still and warm as possible. No mobile phones then, only phone boxes, but there was one nearby. The ambulance came pretty quickly and they took him away while the police cleared up the mess, asked us for witness statements and eventually cleared the bridge. The driver didn't say much for the rest of that day. He had a son who had a motorbike.

On another delivery trip I saw Barry Theobold, standing on a corner in the suburbs waiting for someone. That was a surprise, he told me and some others that he'd gone to train with some Chinese man overseas for six months, but had been in Leicester for about three months! Barry was one of the GY "Characters" and although a bit OTT sometimes, a likeable chap.

"Yarmouth!"

One night we'd been to a pub where they had Jazz jamming sessions and were walking back towards Silver Street along this back lane with high walls either side. We heard a gang of lads approaching who were chanting some football slogan. Like "Chelsea, cha cha, cha, cha!" For a start, I had problems with imagining a football team doing a Cha Cha, but they seemed to be engrossed in the idea. So they kept chanting as they got closer and the sound echoed around the high-walled streets. They were getting closer. As seven of them came around the opposite corner, Tony said to me "Oh gawd! What do we do now?" A quick think and I told him not to worry and just follow my lead. I said "Cross over" and we crossed over to the same stretch of pavement that they were heading our way on. Then I started clapping my hands fast and heavy, chanting "**Yarmouth!** (clap, clap, clap)" with Tony and Ricky joining in. We stared straight at them and headed straight for them. They crossed over. Much to our relief. That could have been a disaster if they hadn't.

In the Ill Rondo one Saturday night we were all having a good time. Some of the Jamaican lads were in there, and their girlfriends, who danced with all of us. I went to get a pint and some drunken lout bumped into my arm. Turning quickly, as you do, this fool who bumped into me then accused me of bumping into him and spilling his drink. He had an almost empty glass. Before I could even open my mouth, 'Junior' one of the Jamaican lads, literally danced across to us and said to the lout "Here, what you doin' with my mate from Great Yarmuff man?" and the bloke instantly changed his tune, apologised and offered to buy me a pint. I laughed, told him where to go, basically, and not to try that again. Our pal Junior was usually on-the-ball and also a good laugh to be with. The girls, far from being enslaved, seem to enjoy their lifestyles. There are bound to be fights, wherever you go. Overall, there were less fights per week in Leicester than there were in Gt Yarmouth, so it wasn't a bad place to be at all.

We had an old railway waiting room bench in the bay window of the Flat and would watch the line of cars going slowly down the road each night as, we found out, further along the road was the "red light" area! We had a single bed each, one sheet and one blanket. A shared kitchen and shared toilet with a young couple downstairs. They were alright. All we had at first in the living room, apart from the old hard wood seat, was one of those drop-down sofa beds, the flat ones. Later we got an old Hire TV with a coin slot in it, that could also pick-up Radio such as Police and Ambulance, so we often listened to that in astonishment: better than your normal radio plays, real drama! At one time we had a whole bunch of the lads from GY came down and crashed for the night: I think Bernie, Dave and a few others. That was a sight to see. There were four of them laying across the bed, with another four laying across them the other way! Someone else had the hard seat and could hardly walk in the morning. Tony, Ricky and I were alright as we had a bed each: although with only one sheet, one blanket and old horehair stuffed mattresses they were not that comfortable or warm, especially as we had no heating. At least the lads got a cuppa and some toast in the morning.

Having been in Leicester for the best part of the year, I had settled down and was enjoying work and play. We had got the flat sorted out well enough to meet our basic needs, there was always somewhere to go in the evening, if you wanted to, and the locals were pretty friendly. At one point we chipped in and rented a Television set which you had to put coins into, like a gas or electric meter. We chose one with a VHF Radio built in. This could pick-up all the local police, ambulance and fire brigade channels. Believe me, that was far more entertaining than any TV or normal Radio show. Occasionally we even got to hear what was going on down at the other end of our road, like some prostitute stabbing a client who had refused to pay, then giving the old bill a hard time: they loved to tell them at the other end of the radio what was happening, like some bizarre sports or news commentary!

Things were about to change again. No contact had been made with my parents and one day a letter arrived for me. It was written by my mother. She told me some bad news that was about to change my life and pull me away from Leicester for good. My father was ill. She asked me would I come home and see him as he was too ill to work and was too weak to drive. Little did I realise that this was the last chance I had to see my father. A very good man, great father and probably the best friend I ever had; not that you realise it when you are young and having "carefree times".

The coach journey home was long, uncomfortable and the weather was not good either. Cold, foggy, icy patches and even snow or sleet. The journey started early in the morning and finished late in the evening, due to various stops and delays.

When I did get home it was one of the rare times that my Dad gave me a hug. He looked thin, drawn and very weak. Being the trooper he was though he was still working, but only Part Time, and that was hard enough for him.

My Mini Van was long gone. I needed another car, so my father, bless him, called on one of his mates who ran a car sales place on Northgate Street. One day my Dad said he wanted me to go look at a car with him. It was a 1958 Austin Metropolitan. Black and white, with this crazy sort of continental look about it, especially the white-wall tyres and spare wheel mounted on the boot. I guess my Father knew my odd tastes by then and had thought I might like this sporty looking car. He was absolutely right, I did. I Like cars with a bit of character. I later found out just how much character the Metro had.

Mod Metro.
My father introduced me to his friend and I started the car, sat in it and admired the long front bench seat, valve radio (crystal clear sounds!) and the overall looks of the car. The spare wheel mounted on the back was an eye-catcher. Within five minutes I had agreed to take it and handded over the £35 to the garage owner.

The keys and LogBook were handed to me two days later after getting it registered and insured. MCL 832 was now mine. As you can see from the picture, I "pimped my ride" a bit by adding the proverbial "go faster stripes" and racing mirrors. A Fog and Spot lamp, mounted in frontof the grill, made it look the business. You might well ask "Why do that to a 1958 car with a mere 1500 BMC C-Series engine?" Well, one day I wa son my way to work and a 2-to-10 shift - I'd gone back to Birds Eye again - and had to stop in the market p[lace, to give-way to traffic coming around from Burtons' direction. Two young women on the pavement by Nicholls Restaurant were smiling and looking me, so I smioled back. Then heard a "beep" from behind me and relaised that I needed to shift. Not used to the car, I revved perhaps a bit too much and dropped the clutch a bit too easy. Next thing I knew the bonnet seemed to rise up about three feet and the rear wheels spun like crazy, squealing as they did so. The car shot forwards at an alarming speed. I had never driven anything like this before! What was it?

My father looked at it the next day. We raised the bonnet and hew saw this large Pan Filter and said "Ah! That's it then, a Zenith Triple-choke Downdraught Carbouretta!"
"WHat?!" I asked, as it was all meaningless to me.
No more to do, my father asked removed the pan filter to reveal a large gaping air tube going down into the Carb, about the size of a coffeee mug top. He told me to hold my hand about two inches above this hole while he revved the car. I did, he did, and my hand was sucked onto the Carb with quite some force. "What the hell?!"
He then explained that the car must be tuned-up, as nobody would put a Racing Carb on a standard car, so therefore, he deduced, using his vast knowledge of Motor Engineering, that the engine was "reworked" and must have a skimmed head, polished ports and high-lift camshaft, etc. He then looked more closely and explained that what was under the bonet was not the original engine, it was a BMC 1800cc that had been fitted

and souped-up.

Boy oh boy, did I have fun in that car! The next shift I was on was "test day". I ran to the clocking off machine, ran out the back door and was first tomy car. Quick start, a big rev and reversed. The tyres screamed and left a trail of blue smoke as I hurtled out of my space onto the road. The road ahead was totally clear, so I selected First, revved her up and dropped the clutch quickly. Again the tyres screamed and smoked, but the bonnet lifted way up in front of me, the front wheel literally off theground by about thee feet or so, like a Dragster! After a second or so of squealing she took off like a rocket and I hit thirty mph in about 2 seconds, tugged rapidly into second gear, and off she went, hitting the 60 mark in a very quick time indeed.... at which point I slowed down as I was unsure of the beast, and peaople had started coming out of the surrounding factories after their shift.

I was back with my ex-girlfiend, a *big* mistake in the end, though we did have some good times and that car was so much fun. There are a couple of memories involving that car that I had better not publish here. Regent Road and Norwich club 'Samson & Hercules' both bring back mixed memories. The latter when I took her and her two "besties" to Norwich one night for a girlie evening out, picking them up at 11. At that time I had a grey "drowned rat" fur coat: it was nylon, very Mod, but looked like straggly silver-grey fur. I recall the bouncer asking me to put my coat in the cloakroom. I refused.

It looked so cool in the UV Spotlight that I just stood there with it shining, like a right poser, for about five minutes, so the girls could see I'd arrived. No, it didn't get messy with the doorman, he just gave up and cleared off. It did get a bit messy later, when I left with my three girls and three drunks would not take go away for an answer. As the Spanish say "Que Sera!"

Brrrm, Brrrrm, Leader of the Pack!
One of my favourite tricks with that car was played with "boy racers". The traffic lights at the end of Yarmouth Way bring back one funny memory. I was waiting to turn right. A new Mini Cooper pulled-up beside me with some lads in. The driver looked at my car, nodded and sneered, probably because off the GT stripes and age. I smiled. He revved his car with an arrogant smirk on his face. I smiled. The lights turned green and I managed to rev her off without too much wheel-spin, and cornered sharpley on the quayside using the "Suicide Knob" that I had fitted: I had too, otherwise sharp corners were almost impossible with the big 18" steering wheel. She shot off like a hare, leaving the mini behind. I slowed down and stayed at 30 mph. There were two lanes over the bridge to Southtown, so he came alongside me, looking a bit pissed off. I smiled. I let him get ahead, just to see where he was going. Southtown Road, heading Gorleston way. Good. After getting to the wood yards, I shot past him, then slowed down again. He was even more pissed off. He overtook me and headed along Gorleston High Street, towards Lowestoft. I couldn't believe my luck. The lad in the back of his car was looking out of the back window and egging him on, reporting my position. I smiled. We eventually hit the dual-carriageway to Lowestoft. He accellerated and eventually got up to around 85 mph, so my speedo said. The anxious lad in th eback was still telling him that I was behind him, egging him on to go faster. The Mini

Cooper reached top speed, I could tell because his speed was constant. I waited and looked as though I was struggling to keep up with him. They were all laughing and pointing. Check mirror, indicate, pull out... I hit the throttle and off she went like a rocket again. The looks on those lads faces as I shot past them was a joy to see. I smiled, and waved. They were soon far behind me, no doubt crying.

One evening Sandy (Mick Sanderson) was in the Chalet with another lad. Sandy had been a close mate since about 1964, and another of the early Scooter Boys. By then he had a MGB GT, that sort of weird tomato soup coloured one. He was sitting just to the right, inside the door. "Hey Sandy." "Hello Lucky."

"Would you do me a favour mate?" He asked what. I explained that my car was "a bit odd" and that the speedo wasn't workingproperly, as it went past 90 mph (the last number on the clock) and then "knocked" against the zero pin, but from the other side. He agreed and we set-off along the dual-carriageway. I accelerated and Sandy kept behind me, until my needle passed somewhere around the 95 mark, but I was concentrating on the road, as you should do. A quick glance in my mirror by Hopton showed me Sandy slowing, indicating and turning back. I had no idea why. I continued to Lowestoft, went down The Ravine and came back.

When I got back to The Chalet, Sandy and his pal were sitting in the same place again with a fresh coffee. Sandy was really grumpy with me, called me a **** and said he thought I was winding him up. He loved his MGB GT and thought that I was trying to show him up, his mate told me. Then I explained that I genuinely had no idea what speed I was doing and that was why I'd asked him to check it out. His mate said they were doing over the Ton (100 mph) and I just kept pulling away from them!

The MGB GT was an improved version of the popular MG sports car. Although acceleration of the GT was slightly slower than that of the roadster, owing to its increased weight, top speed improved by 5 mph (8.0 km/h) to 105 mph (169 km/h) because of better aerodynamics. At the rate my Metro was pulling away, this means I must have been hitting over 115 mph, and I was still accelerating. Wow! Poor old Sandy,no wonder he was not amused.
One night, knockingoff from Birds Eye, a workmate wanted me to drop him off at Burgh Castle. My girlfreind (the one I'd got back together with) lived in Mill Lane,Bradwell, so I said yes. He was terrified as we sped through the back road (now Harfreys) and to the main Burgh Castle road, which at that time had a hump-back railway bridge. There was a bit of a right-hand turn on the other side of the bridge, the car took off and as I landed I had to twitch the wheel rightwards, then accelerate like mad. I dropped him off - he was out of the car like shot - and headed back for Mill Road. Parking up opposite her house, then waste-land, I noted that the journey had taken about ten minutes, from Birds Eye! My father was right. He was acrazy man on wheels and so was I.

It was the following year my father was on his way out. Not that I really knew it at the time.

The Mod era faded out, at least for me, and after getting married (or "marred" as I call it!) in 1976 and having kids from 1979, life just took different turnings than from the olden days of Modernism and Scootering fun. Eventually, I lost touch with all my old friends, except Lenny and Sue Hodds, Brian and Hazel Harden, Pewee and Steph Rouse, occasionally going into the Talbot where the early 70's crowd used to hang out – they were great days too. We had some great nights in The Talbot, with Pete and Marion behind the bar. Fond memories of The Talbot, as many of us do.

Years pass. Kids grow. They become adults. Another marriage, then more trials and tribulations, sorrow and eventually Severe PTSD, caused by my second wife and events pertaining to... but then, 2013 came along. That was one of those "Who'd have ever thought it?!" Moments.

If Only!
What I never understood as a lad, I do now. Too late, of course. Someone I was talking to after my first marriage broke up said "Women are nest builders my boy. You are only there to provide for them." He likened the relationship to the birds and other animals we share our world with, the male is chosen for his prowess, or ability to show off fine feathers(!) Whilst the female chooses a nest site. He then has to work hard to provide sticks, moss and "fluff" to line the nest with. She then lets her hormones rage and demand babies, lots of babies. The human race is however a bit frail, fraught with psychological problems that most wild animals don't have. The human female is rarely ever satisfied, either with her nest or her partner. Unlike most wild animals, who stay together for life, the human female flits from one male to another: not all, but a large percentage do. Hence we have many broken marriages through infidelity. Many human males are the same and just don't seem to be able to get over that mating ritual. I've never had a problem with that, but I have been caught in the nesting

trap, so to speak. I like the wild-life version, personally, find a good mate and stay together for life. That's what I thought marriage would be like, but learned the hard way. Did you know that if you take the "I" out of marriage you are left with "marred"? Marriage is a mediaeval concept created by the Catholic Church, then propagated by the Church of England. It ties people to the church and the government. A very subtle manipulation indeed, and one which plays on human emotions.

Here we are, many years spent trying to bring up kids to be decent and intelligent humans, but then - like most parents - getting the shitty end of the stick handed back, but knowing better. Again, the wild animals have got it right "You can fly, feed and fend for yourself. Bugger off!" :-D I love my kids, but they certainly try my patience. All I can do is bite my lip, then wait until their kids hand them the shitty end of the stick. But then we just nod, smile and give them a hug.

Who would have thought it eh? After many, many years being dragged through meat grinders by ex-partners who have caused unnecessary troubles, Severe PTSD and of course financial issues, I'm back to being a Mod again, young (well, at heart at least!) free and single.

After so much bad stuff, I must say that it has been an absolute thrill to meet up with many of my old mates from the "good days" and rekindle some of those better memories. They were fab, fun and free times. Just look at the smiles these Mods have.

Sometimes I think back to the relationships I had in the 1960's and how uncomplicated they were, or "appeared" to be. It could be that somewhere, lurking in the girl's subconscious, was the desire to pick a nest site. Generally though they were like friends, some closer than others. Of course we had feelings, needs and the dreaded hormones, but most outings were just walk, chat, go for a drink kind of encounters. Sometimes you'd just happen to catch each other's eye, then stare deeply into them, then the old passions would arouse and the kissing began. It may be me, and the so-called "luggage" that we accumulate through being used and abused in some relationships, but nowadays feels distinctly different and I for one cannot tell what women want or think, neither do they seem to communicate. Although I must admit, being both older and wiser I have managed to avoid a few potentially tricky situations, like the one which arose in a local pub. There were around five younger women (25 to 35), four with kids but divorced, and one who seemed single but "odd", shall we say. That little event culminated in the old green-eyed monster inside the single one when I tested and cracked the ice. They all had a fall-out with the green-eyed one and some left the pub, as did I for safer grounds! It's nice to be older and wiser. ;-)

What's Love Got To Do With It?
What's love but a second-hand emotion.
You must understand
Though the touch of your hand
Makes my pulse react
That it's only the thrill
Of boy meeting girl
Opposites attract

It's physical
Only logical.. Etcetera., As Tina Turner sang in her hit song from 1984.

True love is what makes you happy. It's what you feel inside. This is something we discover by shock when we are young and fall in love for the very first time. Then maybe some expectations creep in, or maybe failed expectations if she secretly feels that her dreams of nest building are not being fulfilled.

Feeling The Love.
One thing is for sure, I fell in love with the Nineteen Sixties, the Mod era, with it's superb music, crazy fashions, Italian Scooters and of course the friendships that came with it. Go anywhere, meet Mods, have instant friends.

(Pic: Taken from 2015 Scooter Rally in Gt. Yarmouth.)

While my course changed dramatically by the end of 1967, my hidden destiny stayed unknown to me. Then in 2013 "Boom!!" It all changed again. After awful times with family affairs a single conversation with my old drinking buddy Kev. While I may have alluded to my old pals elsewhere in this book, I would just like to repeat it again here. "Thank you one and all for the revival of memories, the good camaraderie, the laughs and ride-outs that have all helped in producing this small book. I really hope that it makes you smile, keeps those treasured memories alive and maybe inspire some of the younger generation to go out and be future Scooter Boys & Girls."

Chapter Six.

1968 – The Grim Reaper Strikes.

It was the following year my father was on his way out. Not that I knew it at the time.

It was only a few days later that mother was out, working her part time job at the Northgate Hospital, and I was making a cuppa in the kitchen. My father went to the bathroom. After a few minutes I heard him call for help. He was propping himself up by leaning on the sink and Cistern and could not move. After getting him back to bed I called the local Doctor, who to my surprise said he'd be there within four hours! He and my father knew that they had given him four years to live with a blood clot that was heading for his brain. We were not told, so it came as a shock.

That was around September the 7th. The hospital doctors said that he may only survive another two to three days. He laid in a coma until January and a day after my birthday; I have always felt that this so as not to spoil Xmas and my birthday. Bless him. Naturally, mother was in pieces, so was I.

It was really upsetting to see my father in such a state of ill health. He had always been such a strong, healthy and independent man. It was the smoking, red meat and salt that really killed him, as these had damaged his body so badly that they could not operate.

This was the marker point for me which said "This Way ->" and so with a heavy heart, I thought deeply about the values of life and decided that now was the time to take life seriously. During that brilliant Mod era I had lots and lots of fun, laughs and good times with all my friends. One of the changes made came from a Newspapaer called "Seed". This published aspects, facts, figures and even medical advice regarding all types of food. Articles on meat made me think of my father, and think more seriously too. On the turn of 69/70 I became Vegetarian and never looked back.

Like any sad story though there is always a silver lining. My father left me a legacy, one that I would never forget and endeavour to live by: Be kind to all you meet. Treat all as equals. Try to get to know their story, however small it might be. Never strike out at a woman in anger, just stay calm and refuse to get drawn in to their arguments; which usually stem from insecurity, I notice. Perform your trade as well as you possibly can, for it is your path in life, your support, and should always *be* what is in your heart. He never criticised me, as far as I can honestly recall. He never encouraged or discouraged me either. However, when I did something that I was proud of, then a smile and a handshake would let me know that he was proud of me too. Most of all, he faced whatever was put in front of him with a sense of duty, both to his family and himself.

When I was about 10, I returned home from school one day, cold and tired. My mother told me to go sit by the fire in the front room. When I did that I noticed a new brass Fireside Set. Unusually though, the brass handles were not sailing ships, or other common designs. They were a Snake & Crane, entwined in combat. The sight of these gripped me in silence and I knew that it some deep, significant meaning, both in life and to me, but being young, I had no idea what. It represented what I thought at the time was a "futile struggle", as both

were equally restraining the other. Over 40 years later I found one in my father's old tin, alongside other mementos. He had obviously noted that the symbol was of significance to me and had saved one! Perhaps my father was as spiritual as he was pragmatic?

The symbol represents the origins of T'ai Chi Ch'uan, or "Taijiquan" as it is more often spelled nowadays. The so-called Founder of this most famous Art was one Ch'eung Sam-feng (Changsanfeng) or "Five Peaks Ch'eung"! He was born in 1247 and later witnessed the fight between a snake and crane, inspiring him to use the snakes soft and supple movements in a self-defence system, moulded around the Taoist philosophy, using "soft" or "internal force" rather than external force. This was an indication of my Tao.

1969 - Turn, Turn, Turn.
The Mod era faded out, at least for me, and after getting married (or "marred" if you take the "i" out of it!) in 1976 and having kids from later on in 1979, life just took different turnings than from the olden days of Modernism and Scootering fun. Eventually, I lost touch with all my old friends, except Lenny and Sue Hodds, Brian and Hazel Harden, Pewee and Steph Rouse (RIP), occasionally going into the Talbot where the early 70's crowd used to hang out – they were great days too. We had some great nights in The Talbot, with Pete and Marion behind the bar. Fond memories of The Talbot, as many of us do.

Years pass. Kids grow. They become adults. Another marriage, then more trials and tribulations, sorrow and eventually Severe PTSD, caused by my second wife and events pertaining to... but then, 2013 came along. That was one of those "Who'd have ever thought it?!" Moments.

If Only!

What I never understood as a lad, I do now. Too late, of course. Someone I was talking to after my first marriage broke up said "Women are nest builders my boy. You are only there to provide for them." He likened the relationship to the birds and other animals we share our world with, the male is chosen for his prowess, or ability to show off fine feathers(!) Whilst the female chooses a nest site. He then has to work hard to provide sticks, moss and "fluff" to line the nest with. She then lets her hormones rage and demand babies, lots of babies. The human race is however a bit frail, fraught with psychological problems that most wild animals don't have. The human female is rarely ever satisfied, either with her nest or her partner. Unlike most wild animals, who stay together for life, many of the human female flit from one male to another: not all, but a large percentage do. Hence we have many broken marriages through infidelity. The "other man" of course is just as irresponsible in his behaviour. Many just don't seem to be able to get over that mating ritual. I've never had a problem with that, but I have been caught in the nesting trap, so to speak. I like the wild-life version, personally, find a good mate and stay together for life. That's what I thought marriage would be like, but learned the hard way. Did you know that if you take the "I" out of marriage you are left with "marred"? Marriage is a mediaeval concept created by the Catholic Church, then propagated by the Church of England. It ties people to the church and the government. A very subtle manipulation indeed, and one which plays on human emotions.

Here we are, many years spent trying to bring up kids to be decent and intelligent humans, but then - like most parents - getting the shitty end of the stick handed back, but knowing better. Again, the wild animals have got it right "You can fly, feed and fend for yourself. Bugger off!" :-D I love my kids, but they certainly try my patience. All I can do is bite my lip, then wait until their kids hand them the shitty end of the stick. But then we just nod, smile and give them a hug.

After so much bad stuff, I must say that it has been an absolute thrill to meet up with many of my old mates from the "good days" and rekindle some of those better memories. They were fab, fun and free times. Just look at the smiles these Mods have.

One of the ride-outs in 2015 when the Anchor Gardens were covered with Mods again, and this time Scooters too. That's an improvement!

(Below.) The making of the documentary "Living In '66" by BBC's Radio One DJ Steve Lamacq. That was a good laugh. The video can still be found, if you know how to search for it Fb, Chalet coffee Bar, select "Videos" on the page menu), and I do believe that one or two people have recorded copies.

(Above.) Another of our earlier ride-outs, this time at Horning, enjoying a hot drink and a laugh as we watched novice holiday sailors trying to "park" their boats.

(Below.) Making new friends as well as reunions with old friends. The good man Andy Richardson from the Midlands Scooter Club 'Todrophenia S.C. Mystery Tours'.

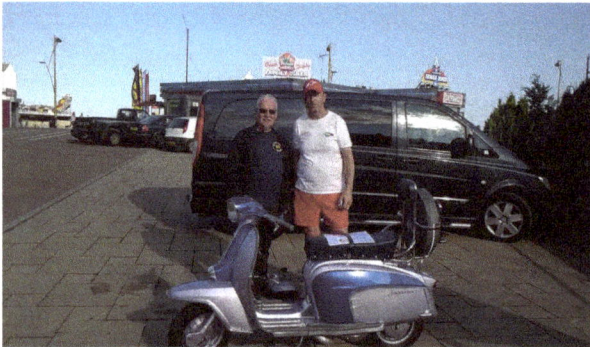

(Next page) Our lovely host at the Chalet, Anne Barker. Without her family keeping our venue alive, it just wouldn't have been the same at all! The Chalet became the meeting place in early 1965, officially, but then continued long after other places had gone. The Bowling Alley, now burned down. Big V, long closed down.

Anne Barker - The Chalet Coffee Bar.

Steve Lamacq entering The Chalet with Steve Streeter - Norwich Rocker in "Living In '66" BBC documentary. Steve was one of the "Three C's" lads: Three C's being the coffee bar at the Charing Cross Centre in Norwich.

Intrinsic?

Is it intrinsic, deep rooted, engrained? Yes. The sixties was our growing up time, a time of much fun, new and long-lasting friendships, and much, much more. Our scooters gave us freedom. They also gave us a chance to express ourselves, hence the designs, paint jobs and accessories. We all have great stories to tell, funny, sad or crazy, but we were there, living it!

Many of the lads agree, young men today just don't seem to have the same kind of spirit, or comradery. Perhaps the future will bring some new recruits to the GY 65 CLUB, and perhaps they will enjoy some of our old adventures and go off to have adventures of their own.

Living In '66:
Graham Hales & John Driver chatting to Steve Lamacq.

(Below) The main group who were featured in the Documentary and who came on their scooters, specially dressed for the occasion. It was amazing to see the piles of photo's that a couple of the

lads had managed to keep all that time and bring along to show the TV film crew. Even more amazing were those tiny little 1960's glass coffee cups that Anne brought out of hiding, you know, the ones you can't even get your little finger through the handle!

We had some good laughs that day. Some of the other lads, shy retiring types that they are, didn't seem to be bothered about being involved. They were also there though: Churchie, Mac, David, and a few more who left early.

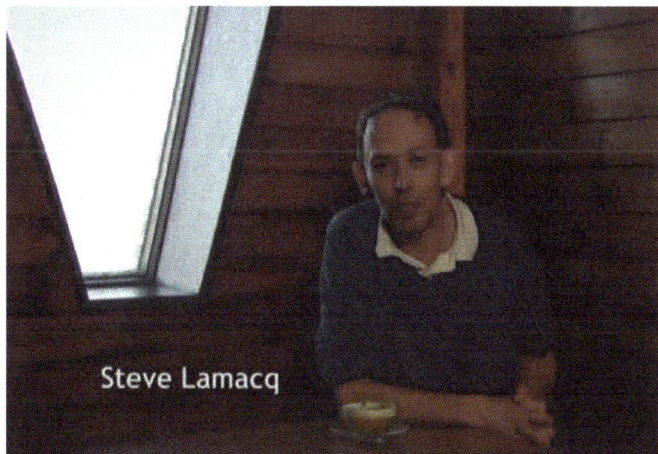
Steve Lamacq

Steve Lamacq, BBC Radio Presenter, making his 'Living In 66' mini documentary at The Chalet Coffee Bar. He was amazed and said "It's just like stepping back to the 60's!" And loved it. The crew brought in a smoke Machine to "make the atmosphere more realistic"!

Facebook pages that you might like to visit:

www.facebook.com/ Search "GY 65 CLUB - Scooters & Mods!"

www.facebook.com/thechaletcoffeebar/

There are many great Scooter related pages on there too, just search for "scooters" for example, and see what you can find.

Chapter Seven.

The GY 65 CLUB

Ask any of the lads who hang-out at The Chalet "Who founded the club?" And you'll get no definitive answer. It seems that, like many things in the 60's, it just happened on a whim. They will tell you that at its prime there probably around 225-250 members. That is phenomenal!

2013.
There I was, in my "local" talking to Kevin and the subject got onto scooters. He said "You do know there's a Rally at Great Yarmouth this weekend?" To which I replied, "Rally? What *Scooter* Rally? Blimey, do they still do them?" On the Saturday I grabbed a camera and drove to GY.

Pictured right is Kevin's "Wildcat", fully restored original racer.

Being August I parked away from the seafront and near the old town wall. Walking along St. Peters Road was the first eye opener: not one word of English was being spoken by the residents. Quite eery as you feel like yo are in another place, miles away. Anyway, hit the seafront and headed for the Diner. There's only one, beside the Joyland Amusements. My heart sang when I saw around 50 scooters parked there. Vespa, Lambretta and a few modern ones to boot, but lovely, multi-coloured scooters. I started snapping and chatting to owners. This one really caught my eye as the paintwork was superb, themed on a WWII aircraft skin, with rivets, parachute pack seat cover, propeller petrol and choke knobs and even War-styled Roundels, but kind of USAF influenced I thought. The owner had spent a small fortune on it, and that was before the price of paints and materials rocketed overnight by around 300%!

That's when I met Peewee, he spotted me drooling and it all revved up and rolled on from there. As stated before, I went down to the Racecourse, where there were many more scooter boys and girls, parked up outside and paid the dues to go in. Just inside the gate were a few of the 60's lads, I saw Pat Weller sitting at a table chatting to some folks. Pat jumped up and proclaimed, in rather too loud a voice "Here, it's Lucky! He's one of the old originals!" This spurred my reply of "Shut-up Pat, I feel old enough already!" We had a good laugh and a chat. It was great to see him again.

Amid the smell of greasy hot dogs and repetitive and rattling Ska Beat - hardly "Mod" - we met up with Mac, Noddy and a few others. It was great to see some familiar faces, even though they were no longer quite the same as they were then

in the mid-to-late sixties. Noddy had a Li "Slimstyle" then and very kindly offered me a seat on it while someone took a photograph, though I'm standing in this one. By the way Noddy, you still owe me a fiver for those oil bottles! ;-) lol Here we are, with Mac.

That little event started a whole new chapter in my life and the life of the GY 65 CLUB.

After Pat told me that many of the lads still haunt the old cafe on certain days, I obviously had to go over there and see what was going on. Graham Hales, Graham Dallymore, Mac, Noddy, John Driver and a few others were regulars. You can imagine how that stirs the memories and emotions that were laying dormant then. Seeing Anne behind the counter (she was Colin's wife and just made the odd appearance in the mid–sixties as Colin and his Dad Alfie used to run the Cafe main, mainly) and the fact that the cafe has barely changed in all those years was just amazing. After a few visits, it transpired that the club was coming up to the 50 year anniversary mark, but there were no plans afoot to celebrate or do anything to mark it at all. My excitement at these reunions spurred the artistic and creative thoughts I've always had, so set about designing a badge: yes, that's right, 50 years on and we didn't even have a club badge! To make sure that we got something that we all liked, I took various designs down to be looked at and commented on by the lads. Eventually one was just right, so 30 limited edition woven badges were made. Here's a glimpse:-

(C)Copyright design-GY65CLUB

This badge now adorns the Parkas, jackets or even kit bags of some of the lads who were lucky enough to grab one. The shape of the scooter outline I made to be a hybrid between Vespa and Lambretta, just to keep everyone happy and avoid any claims of bias. Kidding. The next step was to create a Club Facebook page, so as nobody else seemed bothered, I did it in just a few minutes of my time. If you are a scooter fan, and not already aware of the page, then get on Facebook, find "GY 65 CLUB" and knock on the proverbial door. You can then be informed of any events that may be coming up, and hopefully join in with them.

Memorabilia.

The reunion I planned and pushed for has sparked a whole chain of events, I'm very pleased to say. Graham Dallymore had already helped create a local press article which featured some of the regulars at the cafe. Some bigger reunions were needed, after all, none of us are going to live forever and reunions can also rejuvenate you, enliven the old senses that were starting to nod off, enrich memories with new facts and learn new stories. All this has been done and more. This little book is also a sub-creation of all those events. As I've authored a few books already, I thought it would be really nice to revive some memories and get them down on paper for posterity…. or should that be future generations of scooter loving folks? Anyway, it's here. With help from the aforementioned people at the beginning, Pat, Graham, Chris and Co., We have managed to scrabble together a few odd pictures and memories. Let's go! Let us revisit Memory Lane and enjoy what was, after all, probably the best era in UK history.

Above: Arthur Collins on his Lambretta, possibly at Gorleston.
Above right: GY 65 BOYS, by Harry 'Lord Henry' Manguzi (R.I.P.)

Right: Lita Smith, Jane Swainson and Corrine Frosdick - slightly later on, taken at Backs P.H.

Here's Brian Harden (top left) someone I don't know) then Brian's younger brother Peter: if I recall, I took this as they sat on my Mini Van c.1967.

Brian had a scooter but wasn't fussed about being a member of the club, he just enjoyed riding it. He's back in the saddle, while Pete enjoys four-wheel classic rides.

GY Boys were just that, GY Boys, so we were all mates and still are. No matter which end of town you came from, we all got on just fine.

Below: Peter Allard, Mick Reid and Arthur Collins on Great Yarmouth seafront: c. 1966.

A bunch of GY Mods, including Denis Tuck, on Deneside in Gt. Yarmouth. Nobody is sure of the other faces and their owner's names, but this was possibly taken around late '56 to '66. That looks like an Austin A45 in the background!

Below: Ernie Millar, a popular lad, seen here sitting on his scooter probably outside his house. Below right: Susan Bridges. This picture taken somewhere near the Wellington Pier by the looks of it.

There were many Mod girls that used to hang-out with the GY 65 CLUB lads, but I could not get more photographs of them unfortunately, not named

anyway. Here is one group of lovely ladies (above), but sadly we do not have names to go with the faces. If you are reading this and know any of them, then I'll leave a space so can write the names in. Good luck!

_____

_____

_____

_____

Mick Greenacre, Barry Tough, Martin Burniston and David Downing, on a trip away somewhere.

Above: Peter Allard's lovely Vespa GS with chromed side-panels. This was fairly typical of a Mod Scooter in the 60's, yet each one showed individuality and style with personal colour choices and trimmings.

Above right: Peter sitting on his GS, c.1965. Peter is another of the steadfast "65 Boys" who also became known as "The Chalet Scooter Boys" due to frequenting the coffee bar of that name. Below: My old 'local' mates Barry Green, Brian Church, Mick Sanderson, Ricky Elvin and Arthur Skippen; photo taken by Tony

Elvin. This was on the trip to Taunton that I missed due to work. Not a very good quality picture, but it is 50 years old, so we are lucky to have it!

Alan Hall sitting on his Lambretta GT? Again taken on Great Yarmouth seafront, opposite Trafalgar Gardens.

Below: Henry 'Lord Harry' Manguzi (R.I.P.) in his Parka, again about 1965. We met up again in 2018 at the Chalet Coffee Bar and had some good stories to swap. That's Henry on the left and me on the right, taken about a year or so later, but one of the very few pictures I have from those times. Between 2013 and 2018

Reunions: there have been many happy reunions. The next reunion is planned for August 7th 2020, and Fridays around that date thereafter, at The Chalet Coffee Bar, Gorleston-on-Sea. Be there or be square, as they used to say in the 60's. Although it's primarily the GY 65 CLUB Reunion, anyone who was a "65 Club" member, or just one of the crowd is really welcome.

As I'm running out of pictures, I shall leave you with these.

Addendum & Tribute:

Very sad to hear that as I am finishing this small book of memories, that news has just reached me that my dear friend

Harry Manguzi (left) has suddenly and unexpectedly passed. Like many of the 65 Boys, Harry was a one-off. During the mid-sixties he was one of my riding companions, Cafe mates and good friends. He married a wonderful young woman with whom he fell head-over-heels in love, the equally lovely Adele, and raised a fantastic family to whom our love goes out.
* Also to the others we have lost recently, including Andy Perdicou, Michael 'Sandy' Sanderson, Paul Hainsworth, Mac Powsey, Micky, Dave Williams, et al.

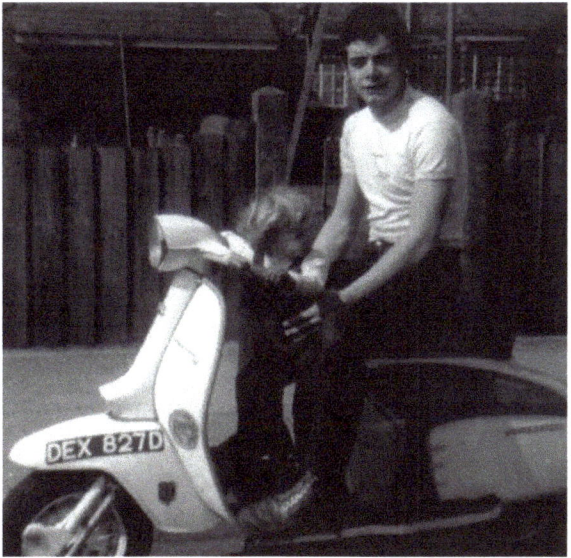

Chapter Eight.

On The Road Again.

The 'Bella!" Story.

From Rags to Riches.
For those who have not met 'Bella!', Allow me to introduce
you. "Bella, Bella, Cinderella!" You might say... well, I just did.
The picture above was the advertising picture taken by an ex-
pat Italian man living in Wimbledon.. Or somewhere around
that god-forsaken area. He brought cheap and abandoned old
scooters over from Italy six at a time crammed into the back
of his large van. Then sold them over here for hefty profits.
This forlorn looking scooter had a rusty tank, was hand-
painted in blue, yellow, green and black, and had gouges all
over the handlebars and very worn seat. An old pal took me to
Londinium in his van to see, buy and collect this weary old
lady who used to live in Milan, the home of Lambretta. To my
surprise the seller had her running, but on a drip-feed bottle
as the tank was fully rusted and had thick red sludge in the

bottom. To be honest, the part in the best condition was an almost new exhaust! However, with a put-put-put she wearily made a special trip up and down the alley behind his garage. Almost two-grand was parted with and then I discovered how the man was not as reliable as his word, or the grand old lady of Milan! When you buy an imported vehicle the seller is supposed to give yo a V40 Import Document. He had said this was alright before the trip, however, on parting with the cash and making sure I got a sales receipt, he made excuses for not having one to hand, but assured me "Don't worry. I'll have one in the post to you tomorrow!" This started a almost three month chain of events where I had to threaten him with legal action and he lied several times saying it had been posted by his wife. This delays plans for a rebuild as you need to have this document before you can get it MOT'd and Registered with DVLA for a new Registration Number. Lesson one: don't trust their word!

Eventually it all came through and I checked its validity, got it registered and then MOT'd - much money and time to pass! The motorcycle repair man had not seen a Lambretta in his workshop before, so that was a palaver. At one point he emailed me and said that the rear light cover would not pass the MOT due to be Italian spec': e.g. had a white plastic centre instead of red. He said "I had to use a black felt marker to go over it, then stick a cheap reflector on it to get it passed for the MOT." What?! I then had to explain to him that it was an original 'Corello' rear light cover and quite rare! Also I had a newer UK spec' cover that he could have used if he'd have kept me in the loop.

The pace was set for continued problems with the rebuild, price-hikes and traders all bringing problems.

After the MOT I had to find someone to strip it down properly, as I neither had the space or tools. It had to be someone nearby as I had no means of transport, so rode it to the nearest Motorcycle Repair Shop in Old Lakenham (no "lid" ala 60's!) this was my first proper ride in... oh, quite some years! It felt good with the wind in my hair. Apart from that joyous little ride one followed private land the MOT place (below), The "strip-down" cost me another £320, which I thought was rather steep as all he had to to was cut-off the rusty bolts. Only the main parts were salvageable, all cables, washers, nuts and bolts were rusted, rusty, or falling apart with age. Replacement parts had already been bought, and this meant many hours on the Internet doing research and finding exactly the right parts:

Lambrettas vary from model to model, year to year. Almost nothing is standard apart from tyres and panels.

The scooter was now just a heap of parts. These I had to get cleaned up and then resprayed. Hence another drama unfolded with that issue. The nearest place I could get a paint job was at Horseford, the other side of Norwich. After a couple of visits I eventually got a quote for £600, which at the time was a bit expensive for scooter resprays as most folk were getting theirs done for around £500. To save a trip to Lincolnshire I said yes. There was supposed to be a bit extra for "blasting" done nearby to this man, but that was thought to have been about £150. However, once I had agreed the price and the colours he said he needed more money as prices of paints had gone up double! Then, to top it all, he didn't do the paint job himself and got some young bloke to do it who then sprayed it the wrong colour. He then denied that he'd made a mistake. All in all, he gave me the impression of being a total cowboy. The finished job was £1250 cash! That hammered my budget badly and the £500 I'd allowed for a respray had more than doubled, the price of parts also went up dramatically, virtually doubling overnight. Eventually, all the parts were delivered back to me.

In my small shed, another expensive purchase, I had already been working on cleaning up the engine. This was caked in mud and oil from the streets Milan and an overworked engine that had not been properly maintained or cleaned in 47 years. It took me three days to clean it, then two more to give it a good going over with a wire brush to get a near original factory look. It was a very long, slow and labour intensive job in my little shed. Eventually it came to rebuild time. Front forks and new ball-races were fist on the list, so Peewee once again "van'd it out" and we went to see Chris Sadd of CS Engineering. Chris is a "old school" Engineer, not "mechanic" and has a trained eye as well as a trained hand. With some "jigging" he fitted the forks and I was ready to go back and start adding the engine and other parts, like cables and wiring loom. Unless you have rebuilt a scooter you have no idea just how much research, then awkward and slow fitting this can be. One of my students, Ian England, helped me refit the engine, tank and exhaust, then cables, etc. Each job poses its own problems and can be quite

frustrating, but it has to be done and done well. Peewee offered to help again and one of his pals helped fit the trim on the leg shields and a few other bits, but got horribly stuck on the wiring and could not get it to work. Back to Chris! He looked at it and quietly pointed out to me that one of the new wires on the loom had been cut too short, plus a couple of other problems, so I had to leave it in his capable hands a bit longer to sort it all out. In the end, Chris found that the old 5 volt system was weak and not without its problems. Off I went again and researched, then bought a new 12v electrical system, new 12v lamps and all. That's a round £180 right there. It all adds up!

Eventually Chris called me and said she's ready to go. As you can see by the picture above, taken in his "Classic Car, Bike & Scooter Hospital" she was looking smart once again. I had already fitted the badges, carrier, and refurbished the original seat, which was unusually a "Giuliari" dual-seat. Lambretta often ran out of parts so bought in anything from makers such as Giuliari or Corello so that they could keep the production lines running smoothly. Originality has been preserved by putting a new, tailor-made cover on it and using all original springs and frame. A new badge was needed though as the old one was broken.

Roadworthy.
The day I went to pick-up 'Bella!' From Chris's workshop was unsettled, weather-wise. A friend drove me his workshop, and I think she was as excited as I was in seeing 'Bella!' Have her first proper run in almost fifty years. As I left his workshop the heavens opened and it rained really hard, so the journey around the busy ring-road home was not a comfortable one!

'Bella!', Italian for "beautiful", is a 1966 Li Special. When these were made they only produced 146,734 of the 125cc models. This makes it quite rare; considering many have been scrapped or written off. Many more have been altered, e.g new engine, so are not original in build. If you are buying a Lambretta, and want "original" then the engine and frame numbers should be near-matching. Both will start with a stamped "LI-S*" (S for Special) then the number. This one begins with 856.... Thus indicating that it was built in 1966 (1966-Li 125 Special - 125 LI-S from 854198 to 867376) and the closest estimate I can make is

that she was built around March 1966. Here you see the one and only Chris Sadd proudly inspecting the bike before it was taken home. My father was they called a "High Class Engineer" and I would classify Chris as being in the same category. He has lost count of the scooters that he has rebuilt, or fixed.

The engine was never stripped, as the budget ran out and it appeared to be running alright. A later visit to Chris proved invaluable though when the gears began "jumping" like crazy and I had a slight wobble as I cornered roundabouts. It turned

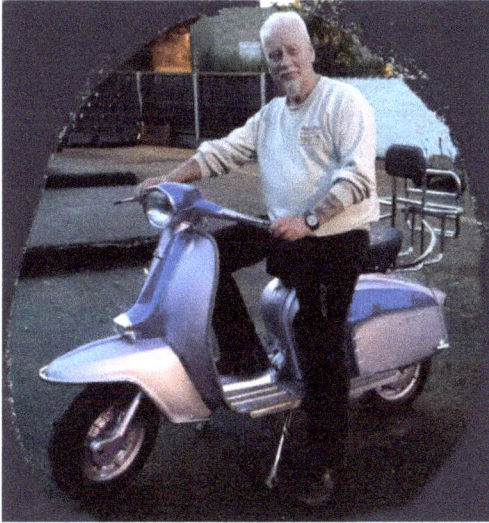

out that the end-plate was loose. He said I was lucky not to have been thrown under a lorry! Hey, I'm a sixties Mod, we don't worry about little things like that! Anyway, that meant dropping out the engine, again (piston rings already done before) and fixing the problem. Final tweaks and she now runs beautifully.

First ride home (above). It stopped raining and the scooter had to be thoroughly dried before being put away for the night. Most people comment on how nice she looks and how the silver-lilac changes colour in different light. The Cobalt Blue is just a stunning colour and the metal-flake helps it sparkle in the sunlight.

When the light shines on the blue it looks like a star cluster!

Wiring Diagram for the 125 Special.

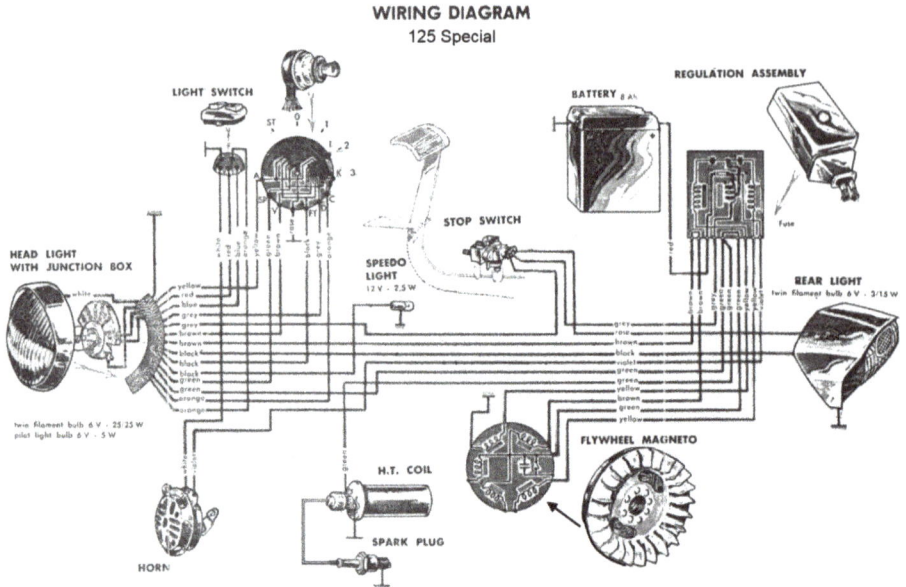

WIRING DIAGRAM
125 Special

Wiring the 125 Special is not too complex, at least not until you get to the main connector block on the headset, behind the headlight. I strongly suggest that anyone attempting to rewire any machine takes a detailed close-up photo before removing any wires. That saved me some hassle.

The theme graphics on the spare wheel cover. The beautiful Monica Belluci, Italian Actress. I chose this picture to represent Italian beauty. I managed to contact her and she gave me consent to use the picture, as mentioned earlier. Excusa me while I sigh... "Ahhhh! Bellisimo!"

The entire rebuild of the scooter took almost two years and went way over the budget by half again! However, as they say, it's better than money in the bank, but only if it is kept "original": e.g. same engine, frame, parts, etc.

Speaking of "original", the original colour was "Azuro" or Sky Blue, but in metallic. This looks quite anaemic, so I decided on a different colour scheme and spent many hours trying different designs and making it a proper Mod scooter. Not many Mods would leave their scooters plain and "unstamped" with their mark. Here was the final design. For this I used a useful PC programme called Paint.Net and some

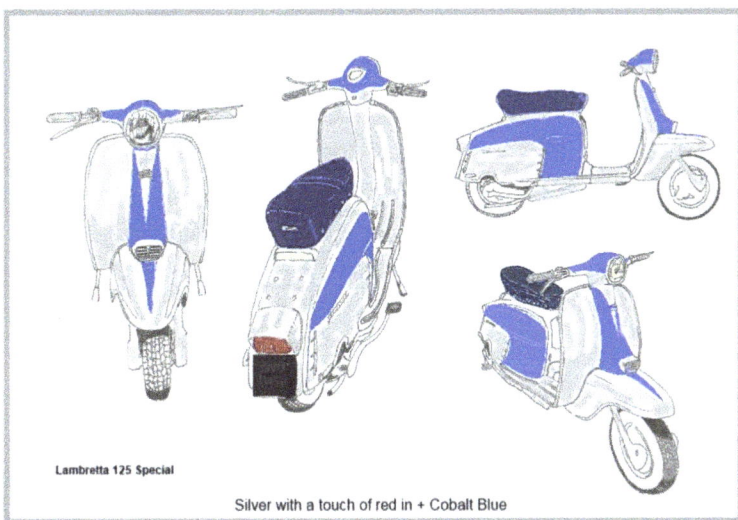

Lambretta 125 Special

Silver with a touch of red in + Cobalt Blue

templates of scooters I found on-line. The nice thing is that in the scooter's design stages they deliberately put extra extrusions on the side panels, horn cover housing and mudguard. This immediately gives options of paint fill or fine-lining that can make each machine as individual as the rider. The whitewall tyres have not happened, yet.

As this is an original Italian machine, not a British import, it does not have a battery holder, or battery. Therefore I thought the final touch should be seen on the number plate. In Milan, during 1966, the number plates where white (we can't have white, so I opted for yellow). The number would have started with MI 80, so I added this and the Italian Tri-colour from the flag to the number-plate. That, plus the name 'Lambretta' gives it a really nice finish and a history to be proud of.

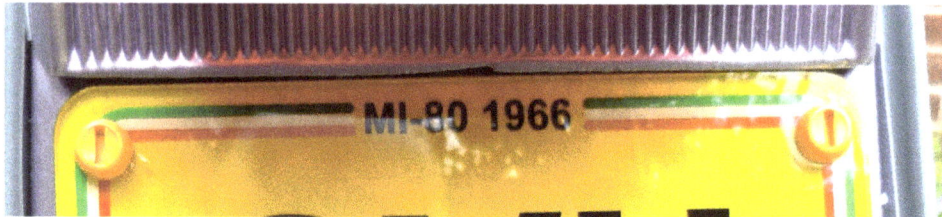

Everyone's scooter is individual, unique to them. So it is that 'Bella!' Is a unique Mod Machine and both a tribute to the Mods and Innocenti Lambretta of Milano, Italia.

'Bella!' At Joyland American Diner.

This has become the stopping and meeting place for all bikers and scooterists, as well as organises Custom Car Shows, etcetera.

Chapter Nine.

Scooters 'n' Hooters.

The Cultural Roots.

This book couldn't possibly be completed without a few extra references to the era of the mid-sixties and some Modrobillia (that's my new word for Mod Memerobillia!)

Posters were the media for selling then as TV was barely established, and also in monochrome, so not as colourful as Art work. In UK most posters were displayed in the few shopps where you could buy a new scooter. In Italy too they adorned walls and gave eager young riders ideas of freedome and escape.

The Lambretta "Jet" was the Spanish made version of the GT200.

In the late 60's, 1969 onwards until 1972, the Lambretta GP became Innocenti's latest fashion statement. A trendy looking oblong headlight and plastic parts appeared.

In Italy beaty queens were sometimes photgraphed with a scooter, Miss Lazio may even have hit the jackpot and won this Vespa as part of the prize!

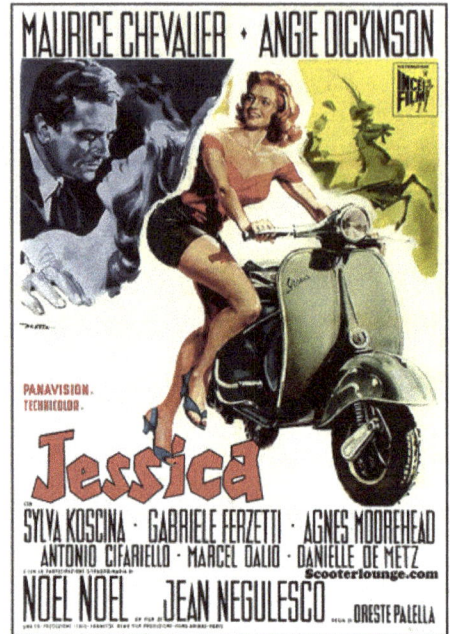

Meanwhile, the film 'Jessica' featured a Vespa..... what? Oh sorry, it featured Angie Dickenson (later 'Wonder Woman') and she rode a Vespa! Both nice, to be honest. Maurice Chevalier was a woman magnet, even my mum used to drool when his name was mentioned. He sang a song called "Thank Heavens (for little girls)", an inoccuous title now banne by the BBC because of the title's possible interpretation. He was in fact singing about how they grow up to be beautiful women, and that was part of a film he starred in. (Below) UK Model Jean Shrimpton was also featured with the trendy J series Lambretta.... blimy, cheer up woman, it is a Lambretta! Where there were good looking scooters, there were good looking women.

Vespa, is Italian for "Wasp", started with a model like this incarnation on the left. Their curvaceous lines were spotted by some eagle-eyed person, possibly a man but you never know, and soon had them associated with the beauty of the human

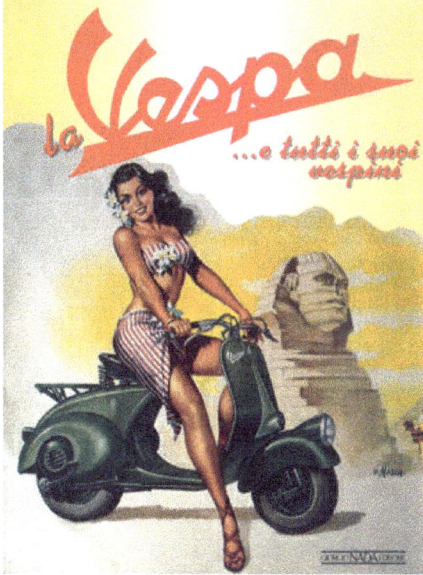

female form and so humble motor scooters became synonymous with glamour and women's liberation: what was frowned upon by former

GEORGIA MOLL CON LA SUA

lambretta

IL MOTOR-SCOOTER DEL SUCCESSO

generations became "the norm" and those women who wanted to celebrate their femme fatale did so with glee. Even today, many women love to pose on a scooter: but not necessarily naked, especially in the British climate!

This poster of a 1947 Lambretta Ld, showing girls have freedom and independance, nipping down to the beach for a swim on her new fangled motor scooter.

Old News.

Newspaper Ad's on the other hand were just black print on white paper. Key features had to sell the product, like the sleek lines of the scooter and the bold Lambretta logo. You may have spotted the "single twin seats"; many original machines had these, up until around 1965, but were replaced by "dual seat" variants.

The Lambretta designs changed slowly, bit by bit sometimes as Assemblers or "Assemblatori" probably suggested how to fix awkward assembly problems.

Aerial photograph of the Innocenti Lambretta factory in Milan. As you can see, this was a sprawling site, giving us some idea of just how popular these machines were and how much space was needed to make them in.

This next shot of just one production line in the sixties shows Li models being prepared for the road; possibly ones that were not assembled properly and had to be maintained. The Li went through many changes in its life, but perhaps the most popular model was the one we called "Slimstyle". No doubt about it, Italian design was sleek and modern.

Timeline of Models:
Model A, 1947–1948 - Model B, 1948–1950 - Model C & LC, 1950–1951 - Model D, 1951–1957 - Model LD, 1951–1958 - Model E, 1953–1954 - Model F, 1954–1955 - TV Series 1, 1957–1959 - Li Series 2, 1959–1961 - TV Series 2, 1959–1962 - Li Series 3, 1961–1968 - TV/GT Range, 1962–1965 - Li Special, 1963–1969 - J Range, 1964–1971 - SX Range, 1966–1969 - Lui/Vega/Cometa, 1968–1970 - GP/DL Range, 1969–1971 (Italy,

thereafter Innocenti stopped production in Milan) - GP/DL, 1972–1998 (Made in India under licence).

Left: Lambretta Special production line being viewed by special guests.

Jayne Mansfield, 60's film star, was hired to promote the new "slimstyle" Li 125 c.c. and Li 150 c.c. models. Later they produced some sportier 175's too. What a beautiful Lambretta, a design I still like to this day.

To me the Slimstyle design epitomised the sleek lines of the Lambretta and the dual-seat added a very distiguished touch. Jayne Mansfiled of course appeared in.... Er, in... Errr? Anyway, Lambretta is by far the most beautiful scooter design, unless you like fat bottoms and wasps.

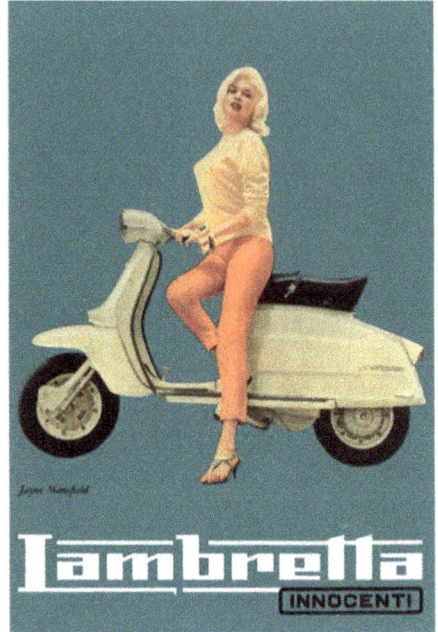

(Below) The Wasp, "Vespa" in Italian. The designers showing off their inspiration here in this illustration.

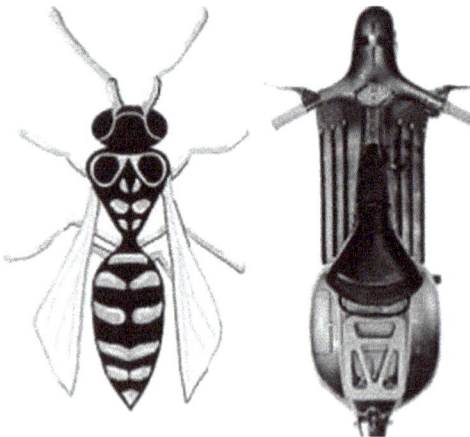

From the very outset though Lambretta realised that women were as likely as men to want to own a nippy Motor Scooter which were also fun to ride, as the poster on the right shows. In this picture the woman is shown on the later model, with higher leg shields that

stopped her skirt being blown up around her waist as she rode! Both Lambretta and Vespa realised that leg shields

...piacere di viaggiare

Lambretta

were useful for keeping most of the rain off too, as well as adding extra protection in an accident.

The design changed quite radically from the original Ld's to the '69 model 'Luna': named after the Moon as Moon Landings were then taking place. Just look at the fuel tank, spread along the top frame and sandwiched under the single seat! This was one radical departure which came at the end of Innocenti's production period.

Lambretta were confined to making Motor Scooters, but when a Motorcycle company said that they were going to make a Scooter, Innocenti replied with this rather radical and, I must say, beautifully styled motorcycle. A 250 cc Racer. It is thought that Lambretta were saying "Well, if you start making Scooters, we can start making these!" The other company dropped its idea and just continued making motorcycles. I must admit, I would really love to own and ride that bike! No other radical departures were made by Innocenti, even though some people made Water-Ski Scooters, or conversions for existing scooters to be ridden on water. I recall in the late 50's that my father had a couple of Water-Scooters in the garage showroom. I used to sit

on them and imagine the fun of skimming across the sea on one. Never have done though. Perhaps that's another one for the so-called 'Bucket List'?

Innocenti did make some very early Mopeds. These have become highly collectable nowadays, not for the style or top speed, obvioulsy.

There has always been a bit of banter going on between Vespa owners and Lambretta owners. Vespa owners come out with things like "Bulit in Italy, pushed in Britain" to taunt Lambretta owners. I thought I'd just publish this picture for a bit of fun and compensation for us poorly treated Lambretta owners. ;-)

Scooters are Two-Stroke machines, needing to have an Oil/Petrol mix, built on a budget and made to be pretty reliable. But like any other machine, if you don't look after it properly it will break down. Common troubles are Brake or Clutch Cables snapping, electrics getting dirty or bad conections over time and, oh yes, running out of fuel because there were no handy fuel guages!

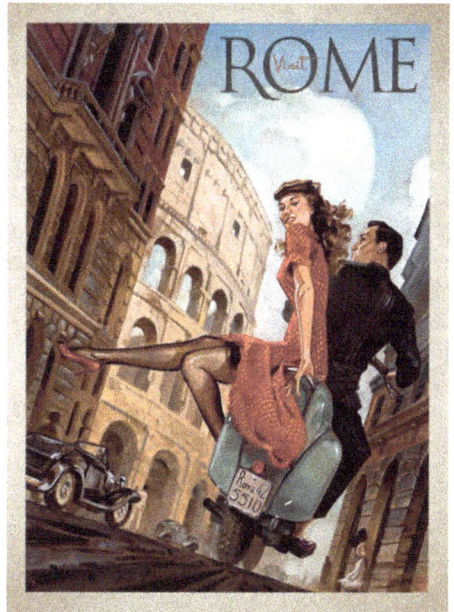

Vespa too never missed a trick in their advertising campaigns. You can see this one says... what, you can't speak Dutch? Oh, alright then, it says "More power and suppleness. Thanks to powerful engine and direct drive. All p.k.s developed by the engine are transferred directly to the rear wheel... (Etcetera)"

Yes, I cheated and used Google Translate! So, they have used a (rather strange looking) picture of a young woman wearing Boxing Gloves to denote that the scooter has more power:

"Punch!" No idea of the exact date of this advertisement, but I'd say late 1950's or very early 60's. I'm sure one or two eagle-eyed readers will spot the Vespa model make and production year.

When in Rome...
Even travel posters featured Italian scooters, like this one (above) which simply says "Visit Rome" and features what the artist portrays as a freedom loving young couple seeing the sights of Rome on a Vespa motor scooter. Bella Italia!

Vespa were probably featured in more Films/Movies than Lambretta, to be fair:
1953 'Roman Holiday' starring Gregory Peck and Audrey Hepburn.
1959 and 'La Dolce Vita', To Catch a Thief (Alfred Hitchcock, 1958), then 'Scarface' (Brian De Palma, 1983), 'The Interpreter' (Sydney Pollack, 2005) and, much more recently, 'The American', starring George Clooney. There are probably a few more that are not listed here, but, pardon the pun, you get the picture. Lambretta seem to be featured more in either Italian movies or later ones like one story about Pablo Escobar (South America). Vespa, made by Piaggio, even used a newer model in the 21st century with a Pope character, no doubt to portray their "heavenly design"!

NOT YOUR **EVERYDAY** RIDE

There's no doubt about it, Motor Scooters really caught the imaginations of millions of people. Even more popular than Motor Bicycles ("Bikes")? Probably about the same. In Italy the humble scooter rose to the fore as the busy and crowded streets made them ideal for nipping in and out or around traffic, narrow streets and alleys. Also the design of the leg-shields, to keep your trousers dry on the way to work, also for the ladies' modesty, proved a popular choice.

This picture, which was in the Public Domain, shows a very nice shot of an Italian street in the late 50's, I guess. No doubt there was a Cafe or Tratoria nearby where riders of any two-wheel machines gathered to chat and drink coffee: where our Mods in Coffee Bars habit came from.

Here is the old Piaggio Vespa factory. Again you can see the size of the operation and the long sheds where the production lines carried parts or sometimes finished scooters along to the next stage. Each line may have worked on a different model: obviously keeping parts from being muddled up together, which would disrupt production. The "Wasp" is still the basic shape for Vespa today

and only changed slightly.

Vespa has made far more models than I care to list here! You can see the complete story on the World Wide Web at

Wikipedia though: search for "Vespa model history".

Vespa did have one unofficial model that they like to list. This was the specially customised Vespa for the movie "Dick Smart, Agent 2007"

This vehicle was used in the movie "Dick Smart, Agent 2007" with Richard Wyler, Margaret Lee and Rosanna Tapados. This is a Vespa 180 Super Sport transformed by Piaggio and the English company Alpha Willis.

This scooter, in the movie, was capable of running on the road, flying like a helicopter as well as being a submarine. In real life a couple of stabiliser wheels would have been handy, especially for landing! Flying cars were invented by the Germans, towards the end of WWII, so why not a flying scooter.

Whatever the choice, the fun was all the same. It was something which brought many people together. Those were different times to know, that's for sure. We can all recall how we could go to any town or city in Great Britain and instantly make friends. See some Mods, they come and talk to you, or you say hello to them. It was that simple. Sadly today's governments and climate have brought about an air of mistrust for strangers. In the sixties there was no such words used as "mistrust" or racist terms, at least by most of us. We just got on with it.

Would it ever last?
We are fortunate indeed that today there are still scooter clubs up and down the country. No matter where you go, you may not instantly see them, but there will be a group of scooter riding enthusiasts who meet up and go out for what we call "Ride-outs". This also happens in India, Thailand, parts of America,

Brazil, France, Belgium and... wait for it... Japan. Yes, there is a big Mod following in Japan that more or less mimics the Mod culture we generated in England in the mid-sixties. Here I shall give good mention to my Facebook Friend, *Yoshi Ojima* (pictured left). He restores and repairs scooters and is a very big fan of anything Mod.

Yoshi sent me a link once to a fantastic video of Japanese Mods in the street. Their scooters were beautiful and they all dressed in 1960's style fashions. The one thing that made me laugh though was when an elderly gentleman walked past one young Mod man and the young man bowed to him. We never did that! Perhaps we should have?

There are many thousands of classic scooters world-wide, most of them still being ridden and enjoyed. In some countries it is considered to be a status symbol to ride a battered old Vespa or Lambretta, while all around ride modern plastic trimmed machines: most of which are far less reliable!

Paulo Bainetti (right) another big scooter fan. His Facebook page is visited by many people every day and is totally scooter related and worth a visit 'Paolo Bainetti Scooter Fan Club'. Here you see him looking as pleased as a kid in a sweetshop, posing with what looks like finished

Vespa machines from the production line, ready to be sold to dealers.

For all your great work in collecting all the great pictures and celebrating our favourite transport - Grazzi Paolo!

The love of scooters is growing sitill. A scooter company from Wales "designed" a scooter to look like a GP200 of the late 60's and got a Chinese company to make it for them. The Chinese company realised perhaps that they could make their own brand, used the same basics but then made it look more like the SX Style Lambrettas of yesteryear; albeit with some modifications. The result is shown here. The all singing, all dancing (it has real brakes and everything!) Non-Scomadi but "some Scomadi" Lambretta rip-off, Royal Alloy; really crap name! Lol

This is something that you either love or hate. It has a high stance, compared to the originals, which may affect it on hard cornering. It is customisable to a degree, colours, side-panels and carrier. It is Four Stroke, not Two-Stroke, so you don't have to panic and carry oil! The electric start is the only method, no

Kick-start, and it has fully automatic gear changing. My mind is still not made up on this "progress" version. Many owners do rave about them though and say that they enjoy their travels on them. That's the key: as long as you are happy, then that's all that matters.

Vespa and/or Piaggio are still trading and going strong. The Indian factory LML have just ceased production in 2018, but they still sell old stock. One company in Berkshire, UK, sell LML scooters and add parts to make them look like older Vespa machines, classics of the 1960's, like the much loved GS models; many of which are still about and being ridden. Again these newer LML's are Four Stroke, have an electric start but alternative Kick-start too. Useful. Pictured here is that rather attractive looking Tasso 'GS160' - actually nearer 200, but it looks the part. At first glance even the trained eye may be forgiven in thinking that this was an original Vespa GS!

Whatever your choice there is a model out there which suits you. Of course, if you want something collectable, then only an original will do, and these do not go down in value, only up! Hence some lucky people have a garage full of Lambretta or Vespa machines which they say is "better than money in the bank".

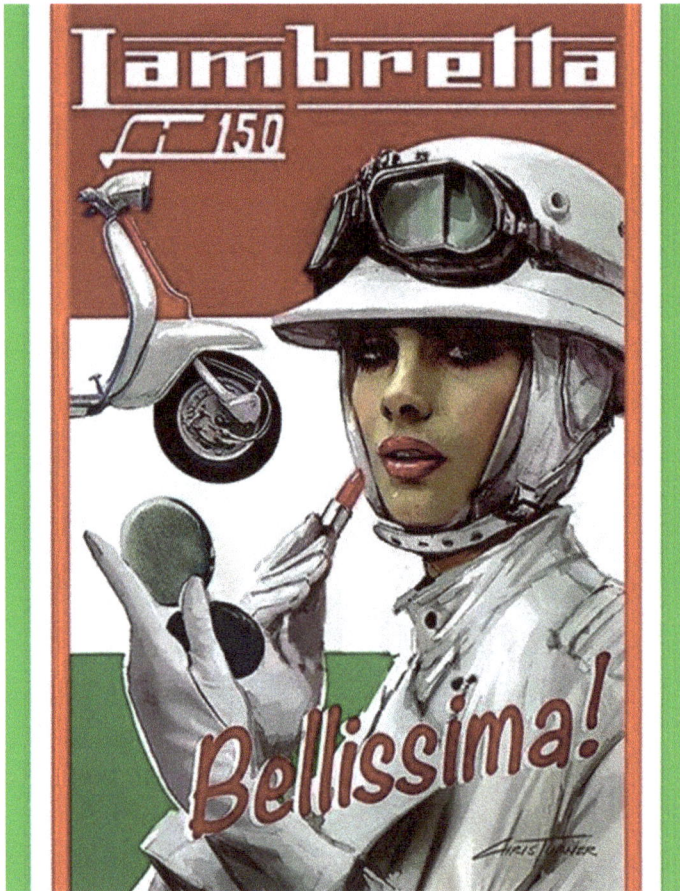

Chapter Ten.

Bella's Adventures!

One of the greatest things about the whole experience of getting back on the road on two wheels again was "mates". Both before and after getting the scooter refurbished has been one after another reunion with old chums from the GY 65 CLUB and of course old mates from the 1960's. As stated in the 1963 chapter, I even caught-up with my old mate Joe from before the scootering days and he even telephoned me from Malta, where he now lives with his wife and family.

We've had some great times, me and 'Bella!', Especially at The Chalet Coffee Bar with many of the "lads" who still frequent the place. And there was me in 2012 thinking that all of that had fizzled away! It did transpire that nobody had made plans for the 50th Anniversary of the GY 65 CLUB, so I quickly bump-started the idea and, as it happens, we all had a great time and that lead to our first big reunion. Here we all are in 2017 outside our spiritual home, where we are also known as "The Chalet Scooter Boys". Current family owner Anne Barker is seated

right. Graham Dallymore (left, standing) has been busy too, helping to revive more memories, contact old club members and also get more publicity for the group. Standing next to him is Alan Virgin, someone we had not seen since the sixties. Seated second from right is Bryan Bream who came all the way from northern Scotland to be at the reunion. Bryan was amazed to find that the wooden spoon he had bought for Colin was still on the wall and the place had not changed since we all used to go the in the mid-sixties.

The infamous wooden spoon, presented to "The Worlds Biggest Stirrer", e.g. Colin Barker, by Bryan Bream (Pictured).

We all had some laughs and some brilliant memories. But that lead to a second reunion the following year when even more of the GY Mods turned up. The next one we are hoping will be even bigger.

Although today's traffic is hectic, faster and more dangerous than it was in the sixties, it has been a pleasure to ride the Lambretta to many places, meet new friends or acquaintances as well as old friends. Wherever you go you get people coming up with a smile on their face saying "I used to have a scooter..." and reminiscing with happy memories.

Below are a few pictures of places where la belle "Bella!" Has been. Nowhere too far, as age and arthritis makes it uncomfortable to ride more than say 25-30 miles each way. When you do get on a quiet country road though, it's just like the good old days, just you and your scooter enjoying the scenery while listening to the delightful sound of a two-stroke engine pulling you along at a steady speed, the sunlight flashing off the paintwork and metal.

One of the Norwich Scooter Collective meets at the Fat Cat & Canary on Thorpe Road. As you can see, not everyone still rides scooters, but two wheels is two wheels, so we're all brothers now.

Great Yarmouth seafront, summer 2017. A ride-out organised by Ian King of Norwich. That was a hot day!

The Chalet, of course. Here with old pals Peewee and Brian. At one time they used to run a Disco at the Royal Hotel which was

very popular. They asked me to go do the middle set and get people dancing and warmed-up for the last set, which I was more than happy to do. We had some great nights there. Like

most of the group, we got marred, had kids, moved and settled down and lost touch completely. Great to see them again. Oh sorry, did I type "marred" instead of married?! Lol

One place that's really nice to be on a sunny day is Ranworth Broad, near South Walsham. Lovely pub there, The Maltsters, the shop and Post office who do a tasty Ice Cream and the little cafe behind that where you can get a coffee or snack. As can be seen, other classic owners go there too. This MG is very complimentary to the Lambretta's 60's styling.

Another sunny day, another meet-up. Left to right: me, John Nockolds, Bernie Shepherd and Graham Dallymore. Another sunny day and ride-out and meet at the diner in GY.

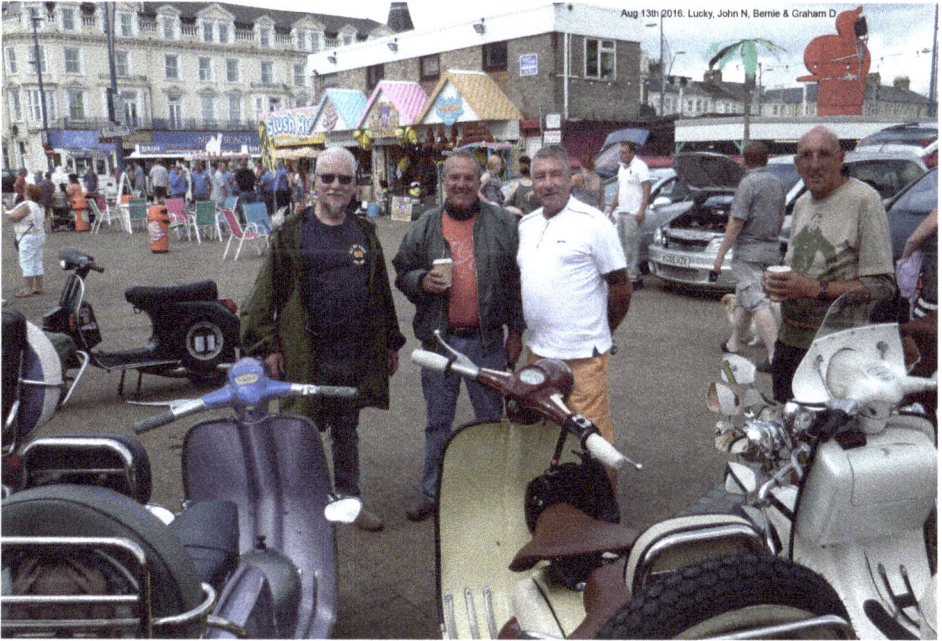

There is always somewhere to go when you have a scooter. The trouble is that nowadays you can't leave it unattended like you could in the sixties as there are so many scum-bags about with vans who will steal it; no regard for the hard-earned money, blood seat and tears that anyone has put into the rebuild.

Here is 'Bella!' Feeling right at home in Wymondham as a steam engine goes past. There I spoke to a man who had a classic Honda motorcycle, plus one of the volunteers who helps keep the Mid Norfolk Railway running. That runs, currently, from Wymondham Abbey to Dereham and is a very pleasant trip indeed. Dereham Station is is a fine building and the cafe there is pretty much the same as it would have been "back in the day" when steam trains ruled the rails. If you avoid Dereham town, it makes for a pleasant day out, getting gently rocked by the locomotion: similar to being rocked gently in the womb and why so many people like rail travel of this sort.

Bella Does Bungay!

Bungay has a feature or two that not many people discover. One is Jester's Cafe, a worthy stop-off point which offers nice food at reasonable prices. Two is just behind there, where you see the footpath on the left. Bigod's Castle has a very interesting history, and if you read it (books available in the cafe) you'll see that nothing has changed in the world of politics and power for many a century!

That particular spot was one I visited many times as it is really nice on a warm day and the courtyard offers shelter from any breeze, street noise and hubbub of the town centre.

The ladies love a scooter! Everywhere that 'Bella!' Goes she gets admirers... I get none! Here's the lovely Joni who used to work at 'River Kitchen' in Hoveton: great place to sit and eat/drink and watch the antics of untrained holiday-makers on little boats or bigger ones! On this day I recall that as I entered the car park three large motorbikes were then leaving. They slowed to a standstill and admired the scooter. It made me wonder why they had big "common" bikes when they admired an Italian work of art?

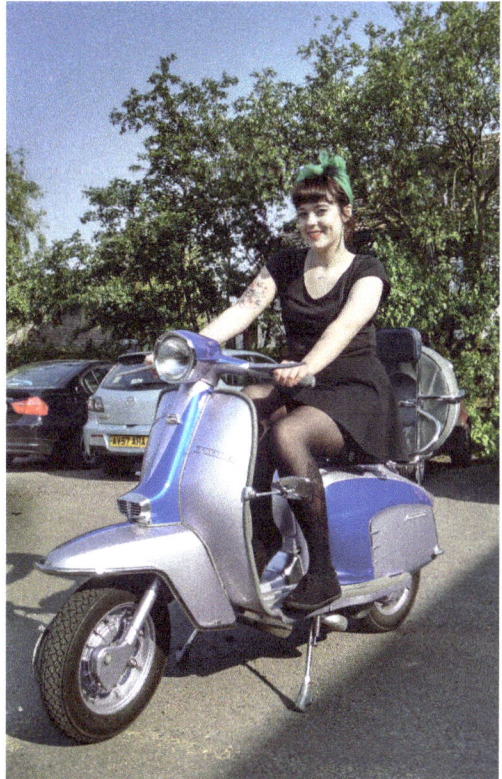

On a sunny day I had been to Gorleston, then GY seafront but it was just too nice to go home and stop riding early. This is how scootering gets to you. The only penalty is having too many coffees or being hit by too many flies!

Here you see "her" at Bradwell Hall, the home of former Staircase Lead Guitarist Kev Claxton: now with 'Jacques de Ladde'. A most suitable location for a grand lady of splendour and good caste.

There are many more locations that the grand lady has been to locally, and more to come, I'm sure. The summer of 2019 will be another summer of fun and friends. Here's one I met earlier. On

a lonely Sunday outing I decided to visit the Diner for a coffee and watch the world go by. As I pulled in, this man, Andy

Richardson and his wife Joan, were standing nearby. Andy came over and introduced himself, his wife, daughter and her boyfriend. Andy belongs to a group of scooterists in the "black country" called "Todrophenia - Mystery Tours". It's amazing how scooters and motorbikes make instant friends.

Lastly, this is where the cover picture comes from (Taken by Michael Keenan - Photographer). Happy rides folks.

No matter where you go in the world you will find Scooters. Wherever there are scooters Mod's will be found too. USA has many scooter clubs, but the one which surprised me most was the extremely 60's Mod-like Japanese scooter clubs.

Below: Before and after. What a transformation, yet keeping it as original as possible.

Below: 'Bella!' Mingles with a classy 60's MG Sports car. The lovely Joni just loved posing on 'Bella!'

SUMMARY.

Boys and girls, thank you for buying this little piece of history. You're not making me rich, by any means, but I may be able to afford a cuppa while at my favourite coffee bar, The Chalet!

It has been such a pleasure writing this book, even though it took a long time and I had many frustrations with memory, and PC software issues. It has taken me six years, but I have travelled back more years than that to a time which was heady with adventure, fun with pals and also the most important part of your life; e.g. "growing up"!

There are some stories that I could not possibly publish due to what we may call these days "snowflakes"… ha ha ha ha! Oh no missus, don't titter. Titter ye not! Seriously though, some stories may have embarrassed not only myself but some of my dear old friends too, so, far better left out.

To my male friends of that great era. I know some have moved on to the next great adventure, but for those who remain and read this, "Whoooo!" I had a hoot. We had such good times and shared such great adventures; for teens back then. To all those I meet up with now, thank you for being here, meeting up and sharing some good laughs and happy memories.

To my female friends of that great era. Sometimes I must have been a bit of a conundrum I guess, not specifically chatting up any particular girls, but just enjoying their company on equal terms. Never had "the chat" anyway and never went out with any unless there was some sort of "spark" as they say. Yes, we had equality. On odd occasions I may have "gone bump in the night" with a delightful female friend, but probably only if you were honest and let me know you wanted me. Otherwise, we just had fun with the crowd. If I'm absolutely honest, I can't remember too many names - not even most of my mates' surnames in fact! However, you all have one thing in common, I love you all and thank you all for being friends. Your company was greatly appreciated and valued.